For 'PKs' Only:

A Book for

The Next Generation

Keith Butler II and MiChelle Butler

Unless otherwise indicated, all Scripture quotations in this volume are from the *King James Version* of the Bible.

Scripture quotations marked AMPLIFIED are taken from *The Amplified Bible,* Old Testament copyright © 1965, 1987 by Zondervan Corporation, Grand Rapids, Michigan. The Amplified New Testament copyright © 1958,1987 by the Lockman Foundation, La Habra, California. Used by permission.

First Printing 2001

ISBN 1-893575-11-X

Word of Faith Publishing
20000 W. Nine Mile Road
Southfield, MI 48075-5597

Contents

Introduction

In this book, we will be talking about a new generation of believers that God has raised up to take His work, His plan and purpose, to the next level and to glorify Him. This "new generation" is a generation of "preachers' kids" (*aka* PKs).

Section I, consisting of Chapters 1 through 3, will deal in a general way with God's will for the believer today, and we believe it will inspire you as a Christian no matter what your age, status, or station!

Section II, consisting of Chapters 4 through 7, is addressed specifically to PKs and parents of PKs. In this Section, we are especially ministering to this segment of believers. However, what the layperson can glean from the insights we offer can only serve to enhance the individual believer, the relationship between clergy and laity and, therefore, the well-being of the entire Body of believers.

Section III, consists of Chapters 8 through 10. Chapter 8 is entitled "For PKs Only Part 2" in which we share seven keys to taking the work of God to the next level. While written to PKs in ministry, the principles contained in this chapter are applicable to anyone seeking success in the ministry.

Chapter 9 addresses the matter of self-esteem for the PK, *especially* PKs in the ministry! The final chapter contains encouragement and exhortation for PKs, and all believers alike, to kindle the fire of their gift or calling and to be followers in the faith of generations past — of those who have blazed a trail before them.

We are giving special time and attention to the singular aspect of PKs because it has been a subject that has been largely neglected in Christian writing. Every one of us faces challenges in life to one degree or another that can affect whether we take our place in a generation that's glorifying God or just give up and quit, going with the flow of the world.

That's what many PKs are doing today. In the face of challenges, they're succumbing to Satan, sin, and the world and are allowing circumstances to dominate them instead of dominating their circumstances. Some of the challenges that PKs face are unique to them because they've grown up "on the other side" of ministry. Having grown up in a minister's home ourselves, we feel it would be unfair not to address through this medium some of the issues faced by those who are growing up or have grown up in a minister's home.

Many PKs grapple in childhood with what is expected of them — what is expected from parents, from other Christians, and even from God. And Satan is not there to help! No, he knows that these children have the potential for greatness, for being mighty seeds sown in the earth. And he wants to hurt, hinder, and even destroy them. Preachers' kids need to know Satan's tactics and schemes to avoid the pitfalls and traps he will bring their way.

The bottom line is very simple. Satan knows that PKs have the unique privilege of taking what good things they've learned and using them to further the Kingdom and to bless untold numbers among their peers. PKs have the potential for using knowledge at a very early age that most people don't obtain until later in life.

In some ways, young PKs can pose a greater threat to the enemy and his purposes than most other young people. Consequently, there are certain traps that he lays early in life for preachers' kids that, to a degree, have been successful in the past. That's why preachers' kids often have such negative reputations.

But that is changing; that shouldn't be the case with this new generation. And that is the purpose for this book — to help this special generation of believers thrive in the ministry and do all that God has called them to do without faltering or failing.

SECTION I

Chapter 1
Taking it to the Next Level

Rev. Keith Butler II

But ye are a CHOSEN GENERATION, a royal priesthood, an holy nation, a peculiar people; that ye should shew forth the praises of him who hath called you out of darkness into his marvellous light.
— 1 Peter 2:9

The world labels people. It may not be right or fair, but that's just the way the world is. For example, a politician who doesn't spell or pronounce a certain word correctly is labeled as "dumb" or unintelligent no matter what degrees he's earned. A basketball player who makes a mistake and has a heated disagreement with the coach is labeled as a "hothead" for the rest of his career. A person who has a "run-in" with his boss one time is usually automatically labeled as "contentious."

But then, you might get to know some of these people and find that they have been mislabeled — so much so that you don't even know what those who labeled them are talking about! Very simply, it's the nature of the world to label people according to what they think they see or know about people and how they feel about them.

The world labels generations too. For example, most of us have heard of the "Baby Boomers." This is the generation of people born in the United States during a drastic increase in the

1

birthrate following World War II up to about 1960 to 1964 (depending on what demographics study you read). Baby Boomers have been labeled, discussed, and studied. We often hear about this generation referred to in the news even today.

Following the Baby Boomers were the "Baby Busters," and after that, there was what the world called "Generation X" in the '80s who became "Twenty-Somethings" in the '90s.

In this day and age, a new generation is rising, a generation that is increasingly being labeled as troublemakers (even if "unofficially"). This next generation has been characterized as one that is worse than any that has come before it, and understandably so. There has recently been a drastic increase in the amount of violence in school, with school shootings becoming regular occurrences. There's also been an increase in teenage drug use, in "gang banging," and the like. The world, being motivated by Satan and deceived by his misinformation, is raising a generation of young people who have no knowledge of God and, therefore, have a total lack of restraint — a generation of perfect "puppets" for Satan to use to carry out his will in the earth.

However, the world has made a mistake in labeling this upcoming generation the way it has. While it is true that the young people in the world are getting worse and worse, it is also true that any time Satan sets out to do something, God always rises to the task of stopping and defeating him. Isaiah 59:19 says, *"...When the enemy shall come in like a flood, the Spirit of the Lord shall lift up a standard against him."*

You see, Satan isn't the only one raising up a generation. God is raising up a generation of His own — a generation of faith-walkin', devil-stompin', holy-livin', fully dedicated soldiers of the Cross of Christ! It's a generation of believers who have chosen to glorify Him. And when it is all said and done and the people of the earth look back at this generation, they won't be remembering all the negative things that have been done. They will be remembering how this generation rose up and took the world by storm. They will remember how it turned the world "right-side up" because of the millions who became a part of the Body of Christ.

I'm telling you this because you are a part of this next generation, and God has a part that he wants you to play in reaching the world for Jesus. God has a destiny in mind, a purpose, that he wants those of this generation to fulfill. He is calling us to take to the next level what He has accomplished with previous generations. He wants us to accomplish more for Him and with Him than our elders and forefathers did and to, therefore, further fulfill His plan and build His Kingdom on planet Earth.

And that is exactly what this generation will do!

PSALM 112:1,2
1 Praise ye the Lord. Blessed is the man that feareth the Lord, that delighteth greatly in his commandments.
2 His seed shall be mighty upon earth: the generation of the upright shall be blessed.

Psalm 112 talks about a man who is living right before God, a man who delights in God's Word. It enumerates the many blessings that will manifest in his life as a result of his obedience toward God.

The first blessing the Bible talks about is the obedient man's seed, his *children*. It says they will be mighty in the earth (v. 2). For the most part, preacher's kids (PKs) — because of their parents' faithful obedience — qualify, as the children or the *seed*, this verse is referring to.

God has promised your parents that you will be mighty seed and that you will be blessed. That means that God has already given you the ability to be mighty in the earth and to be blessed. All you need to do to make your life everything you want it to be in God is to cooperate with Him. Even if your minister parents haven't qualified as the Psalm112 man or woman, and even if they've missed it immensely in dealing with you, you still can become mighty and blessed if you just stay with God.

The purpose of this book is to minister to PKs so that they can become everything that God has destined them to be. The ramifications of a PK fulfilling his destiny is stupendous, because his obedience will not just positively affect his life, it will affect countless lives with whom he will come in contact.

You see, God has called many of us to be the leaders of this next generation who will lead the charge. It is vital that we avoid Satan's traps and snares and allow God to prepare us for what He wants us to accomplish. God wants to use our generation to usher in the greatest move ever seen on the earth. We have a large part to play in this new "era."

JOSHUA 5:7
7 And their children, whom he RAISED UP IN THEIR STEAD, them Joshua circumcised: for they were uncircumcised, because they had not circumcised them by the way.

In Joshua 5, the Bible is talking about how God raised up a generation of Israelites in the stead of their parents. Most of us are familiar with that story: Israel had been slaves for 430 years in Egypt, and God raised up a man named Moses as the instrument of His choosing to lead Israel from captivity. Moses led them across the Red Sea and into the Wilderness.

When Israel left Egypt, it was a great victory. They not only left Egypt with silver and gold, but the Bible says that there was not one sick person among them (Ps. 105:37). Then God began to talk to them again about a Promised Land that He had for them. Unfortunately, despite the fact that they had seen God work great miracles just weeks before, they did not have the faith to enter the Promised Land.

That brings us to Joshua chapter 5. The previous generation of Israelites, who'd escaped Egypt's bondage, died in the wilderness, and God raised up the next generation, giving them the responsibility of taking the Promised Land.

God Thinks in Terms of Generations

Notice that the Bible says that God raised them up (Joshua 5:7). I want you to see that God thinks in terms of generations, and He does get involved in the process of raising generations. In the same way that God raised these men and women up in their parents' stead, God is raising up a generation of PKs today to fulfill His commission and reach the world for Jesus Christ. In most cases, these PKs will work alongside their parents, but, ultimately, they will take what their parents have done to the next level. As they do, they will succeed in fulfilling the call of God on their lives individually and as a generation. They will take the Body of Christ to the next level.

In the twentieth century, God has used different generations to accomplish different parts of His plan. At the turn of the century, a generation of believers ushered in speaking in tongues — there was a renewal of the baptism in the Holy Ghost in America.

Then in the 1940s and '50s a generation, including leaders such as A. A. Allen, Oral Roberts, and Kenneth Hagin, brought in a great healing revival. And within the last twenty years, we've experienced the "word of faith" movement as a result of what these men and others like them have done. The Word of God has been taught in a way it hasn't been taught before in modern history. Revelation from the Word has dawned on the hearts of men and women in a profound way.

Today we have a generation preaching and teaching the "prosperity message." God is raising up people to teach that. You can see how God uses each generation to do something. Every generation has a purpose to fulfill, and every generation plays its part in causing more and more of the will of God to be accomplished in the Body of Christ. That's what I'm referring to when I talk about the "next level." God is a God who takes us from glory to more glory. It happened in the last century, and it will happen in this one too. God wants the Body of Christ to go to the next level of glory, and He is looking to us to be vessels He can use to facilitate this increase of glory in the earth.

God has certain expectations concerning the generation that He is raising up now. He wants us to continue to fulfill His plan and to do *more* for Him than did generations past. We are to preach the Gospel to *more* people, get *more* people saved, help *more* people receive healing and walk in health, and teach *more* people to walk in prosperity, love, joy, peace, and victory and success.

God wants *more* signs and wonders wrought, *more* of His glory manifested, and *more* people available and committed that He can use to make it all come to pass!

As a PK, I am often reminded of something someone once said to me: "Your parents' ceiling should be your platform. Where they end is where you should take off." That applies to this next generation as well. But for our generation to take the Body of Christ to the next level, this statement needs to be a reality in each of our lives. We're going to look at men and women of God who did exploits — who willingly obeyed God, taking their generation to the next level — and we're going to use what they did and what they taught us as a platform to do even greater exploits and to usher in more of God's glory in the earth. Inspired by our spiritual fathers, we're going to boldly go forth with the confidence that we can indeed do what we were commissioned to do.

Expectations of a New Generation

God wants this generation of believers to take the Body of Christ to the next level. He wants them to continue to fulfill His plan and to do more for Him — to preach the Gospel to *more* people and to get *more* souls saved — than the generation before them.

Let's look in the Word of God at some men of God who associated with someone who was their spiritual father — someone of an older generation who did great things for God. Then we'll see how God used these younger men to take the work of the previous generation to the next level. If you can see how people did it in the Word, then you will know how to do it yourself.

2 KINGS 2:1-3
1 And it came to pass, when the Lord would take up Elijah into heaven by a whirlwind, that Elijah went with Elisha from Gilgal.
2 And Elijah said unto Elisha, Tarry here, I pray thee; for the Lord hath sent me to Bethel. And Elisha said unto him, As the Lord liveth, and as thy soul liveth, I will not leave thee. So they went down to Bethel.
3 And the sons of the prophets that were at Bethel came forth to Elisha, and said unto him, Knowest thou that the Lord will take away thy master from thy head to day? And he said, Yea, I know it; hold ye your peace.

In other words, the sons of the prophets asked Elisha, "Did you know that Elijah is going to go on to glory today?" Elisha responded, "Yes, I know it."

Let's continue reading.

2 KINGS 2:4-7
4 And Elijah said unto him, Elisha, tarry here, I pray thee; for the Lord hath sent me to Jericho. And he said, As the Lord liveth, and as thy soul liveth, I will not leave thee. So they came to Jericho.
5 And the sons of the prophets that were at Jericho came to Elisha, and said unto him, Knowest thou that the Lord will take away thy master from thy head to day? And he answered, Yea, I know it; hold ye your peace.
6 And Elijah said unto him, Tarry, I pray thee, here; for the Lord hath sent me to Jordan. And he said, As the Lord liveth, and as thy soul liveth, I will not leave thee. And they two went on.
7 And fifty men of the sons of the prophets went, and stood to view afar off: and they two stood by Jordan.

Elijah went to three different places — Bethel, Jericho, and Jordan. And at every place, Elisha — the man representing the next generation whom God said would replace Elijah — says to Elijah, "You aren't going anywhere without me."

One thing you must learn is this: You never leave your spiritual father. You just don't do it — not if you want to be a part of a generation that's taking the work of God to the next level. You must follow your spiritual father and his ministry closely and diligently, not halfheartedly. Paul said, *"For though ye have ten thousand instructors in Christ, yet have ye not many fathers: for in Christ Jesus I have begotten you through the gospel* [implying that they had only one spiritual father — Paul]*"* (1 Cor. 4:15).

My natural father, Bishop Keith Butler, has had many ministers on his staff who considered him to be their spiritual father. Yet they became impatient and decided to leave my father's ministry and start their own church. They were anointed men who could teach the Word of God. But fifteen years after leaving, they still only had about a hundred people in their church. They weren't growing. Why? Because the anointing flows from the top. When you get away from the top prematurely, you realize that the anointing you were preaching under wasn't all your own. Unfortunately, for many, that realization comes too late; they never get back to the place they were supposed to be.

I am one of those ministers on Bishop Butler's staff, and I have enough sense to recognize that when I'm ministering, I'm not just ministering with the anointing that's on me; I'm flowing in Bishop Butler's anointing. I'm not foolish enough to leave and form my own evangelistic association just so I can say I'm in charge!

Elisha had enough sense not to start his own "evangelistic association" or ministry. He was already anointed to be a prophet. In fact, he had the anointing to be a prophet for many years prior to Elijah's death. But he didn't leave his spiritual father.

2 KINGS 2:8
8 And Elijah took his mantle, and wrapped it together, and smote the waters, and they were divided hither and thither, so that they two went over on dry ground.

From this verse we understand that Elijah took his coat, wrapped it on a stick, and when they came to the Jordan River, he hit the ground with it and the water split.

Does this sound familiar? Moses did the same thing when he parted the Red Sea. But in Moses' case, it was of dire necessity — he and Israel were being chased by an Egyptian army. In Elijah's case, he just needed to be on the other side, so he hit the ground and went right across on dry land where water had been just minutes before! We can see that this man Elijah was a great man of God.

Let's finish reading about the final moments of Elijah's life on earth.

> **2 KINGS 2:9-12**
> **9 And it came to pass, when they were gone over, that Elijah said unto Elisha, Ask what I shall do for thee, before I be taken away from thee. And Elisha said, I pray thee, let a double portion of thy spirit be upon me.**
> **10 And he said, Thou hast asked a hard thing: nevertheless, if thou see me when I am taken from thee, it shall be so unto thee; but if not, it shall not be so.**
> **11 And it came to pass, as they still went on, and talked, that, behold, there appeared a chariot of fire, and horses of fire, and parted them both asunder; and Elijah went up by a whirlwind into heaven.**
> **12 And Elisha saw it, and he cried, My father, my father, the chariot of Israel, and the horsemen thereof. And he saw him no more: and he took hold of his own clothes, and rent them in two pieces.**

The chariot came for Elijah, and he went up in a whirlwind. He didn't even die; He just "went"! Elisha saw it and was grieved, because his spiritual father was gone.

Elisha Took to the Next Level What Elijah Had Done

Remember, Elijah was a seasoned minister. He had been in the ministry for years. Twenty years before he passed on, he called fire from Heaven. So it was nothing for him to part the waters by the power of God. Elisha had been Elijah's servant for twenty years. He hadn't done any preaching; he was just what we call a rookie. But he was a part of the next generation.

Because Elisha stayed under the leadership of his spiritual father, he started on Elijah's "ceiling." He started out where Elijah left off — and he started by parting the same waters!

> **2 KINGS 2:13-15**
> **13 He took up also the mantle of Elijah that fell from him, and went back, and stood by the bank of Jordan;**
> **14 And he took the mantle of Elijah that fell from him, and smote the waters, and said, Where is the Lord God of Elijah? and when he also had smitten the waters, THEY PARTED hither and thither: and Elisha went over.**
> **15 And when the sons of the prophets which were to view at Jericho saw him, they said, The spirit of Elijah doth rest on Elisha. And they came to meet him, and bowed themselves to the ground before him.**

The sons of the prophets said, "The spirit of Elijah is on Elisha." Elisha had asked for a double portion of the anointing that Elijah had on his life. We know from the Word that the anointing removes burdens and destroys yokes (Isa. 10:27). Well, Elisha wanted *twice* the amount of power to remove *twice* the amount of burdens and to destroy *twice* the amount of yokes! And God gave it to him. God gave Elisha twice the anointing to do twice the works!

Let's look at one other miracle concerning Elisha that happened even after his death.

> **2 KINGS 13:20,21**
> **20 And Elisha died, and they buried him. And the bands of the Moabites invaded the land at the coming in of the year.**

21 And it came to pass, AS THEY WERE BURYING A MAN, that, behold, they spied a band of men; and they cast the man into the sepulchre of Elisha: and when the man was let down, and touched the bones of Elisha, he revived, and stood up on his feet.

Do you see what happened here? A group of men had lost a friend in battle. So they found a tomb to bury him in while they were still in the heat of battle. But when they saw the enemy coming around the corner, they just threw their friend in a nearby tomb and ran off.

The tomb happened to be Elisha's, and the dead corpse happened to touch Elisha's bones. What happened next was spectacular. The dead corpse that touched Elisha revived! This friend was raised from the dead by the anointing on Elisha even after Elisha's death. You see, Elisha took what Elijah did to the next level. He did twice the number of miracles that Elijah had done, and this last one "settled the bill."

Isaac Took to the Next Level
What Abraham Had Done

Let's look at another example of a spiritual son taking what his spiritual father did to the next level. And, in this case, Abraham was not only Isaac's *spiritual* father, he was also Isaac's *natural* father.

GENESIS 12:1-4
1 Now the Lord had said unto Abram, Get thee out of thy country, and from thy kindred, and from thy father's house, unto a land that I will shew thee:
2 And I will make of thee a great nation, and I will bless thee, and make thy name great; and thou shalt be a blessing:

3 And I will bless them that bless thee, and curse him that curseth thee: and in thee shall all families of the earth be blessed.
4 So Abram departed, as the Lord had spoken unto him. . . .

Abraham did what God said to do; he got out of the country. God had promised Abraham that He would bless him and make his name great and that he would be a blessing. Let's find out if that happened.

GENESIS 24:35
35 And the Lord hath blessed my master greatly; and he is become great: and he hath given him flocks, and herds, and silver, and gold, and menservants, and maidservants, and camels, and asses.

How did Abraham become so rich? God made him rich because God said that He would bless him. By the end of Abraham's life, when he was an old man, we see that the Lord had taken care of every area of his life. God had made him great as He promised.

God made the same promise to Abraham's son Isaac — provided that he obey God as his father had done. Abraham had been obedient to God, even when God told him to leave everything that was familiar to him. For Isaac to walk in the blessings that his father walked in, he had to be obedient to God as has father had been.

Let's see exactly what God said to Isaac.

GENESIS 26:1-4
1 And there was a famine in the land, beside the first famine that was in the days of Abraham. And Isaac went unto Abimelech king of the Philistines unto Gerar.

2 And the Lord appeared unto him, and said, Go not down into Egypt; dwell in the land which I shall tell thee of:
3 Sojourn in this land, and I will be with thee, and will bless thee; for unto thee, and unto thy seed, I will give all these countries, and I will perform the oath which I sware unto Abraham thy father;
4 And I will make thy seed to multiply as the stars of heaven, and will give unto thy seed all these countries; and in thy seed shall all the nations of the earth be blessed.

Isaac had to obey God and stay in Gerar even though it looked as if he would be staying in a place of lack. He had to learn how to take a step of faith and obey God without leaning to his own understanding.

Let's find out what happened to Isaac.

GENESIS 26:12-16
12 Then Isaac sowed in that land, and received in the same year an hundredfold: and the Lord blessed him.
13 And the man WAXED GREAT, and WENT FORWARD, and GREW UNTIL HE BECAME VERY GREAT:
14 For he had possession of flocks, and possession of herds, and great store of servants: and the Philistines envied him.
15 For all the wells which his father's servants had digged in the days of Abraham his father, the Philistines had stopped them, and filled them with earth.
16 And Abimelech said unto Isaac, Go from us; for thou art much mightier than we.

We already read that Abraham became great. God blessed him in all things. He was very rich in cattle, gold, and silver. God prospered him greatly. Then Abraham died. Isaac inherited all his stuff and obeyed God for himself when God told him to stay in a land of famine. Then God made *Isaac* great. Abraham became great, and Isaac became *very* great (v. 13).

Abraham once got kicked out of a country because he lied about a woman not being his wife (Gen. 12:10-20). Isaac got kicked out of a country because he had more money than the whole country (Gen. 26:12-16)! There's a difference there. God used Abraham and prospered him the way He wanted to. But then, God took Isaac to an even higher level than Abraham.

God's Ultimate Purpose for David Included David's Son Solomon

I want to look at two Old Testament men you are probably very familiar with: David and Solomon. These two are another example of one generation making things better than the previous generation.

Let's first look at David's purpose.

> **2 SAMUEL 3:17,18**
> **17 And Abner had communication with the elders of Israel, saying, Ye sought David in times past to be king over you:**
> **18 Now then do it: for the Lord hath spoken of David, saying, BY THE HAND OF MY SERVANT DAVID I WILL SAVE MY PEOPLE out of the hand of the Philistines, and out of the hand of all their enemies.**

Abner told the elders of Israel what God's ultimate purpose was for David. God sent David to become king of Israel and Judah. His purpose for David was to save Israel out of the hands of all their enemies.

If you know anything about David, you know he was a man of war. He was the man God used to give Israel victory in battle.

Let's read about the things that David deemed as important.

> **1 CHRONICLES 29:1-3**
> **1 Furthermore David the king said unto all the congregation, Solomon my son, whom alone God hath chosen, is yet young and tender, and the work is great: for the palace is not for man, but for the Lord God.**
> **2 Now I have prepared with all my might for the house of my God the gold for things to be made of gold, and the silver for things of silver, and the brass for things of brass, the iron for things of iron, and wood for things of wood; onyx stones, and stones to be set, glistering stones, and of divers colours, and all manner of precious stones, and marble stones in abundance.**
> **3 Moreover, because I HAVE SET MY AFFECTION TO THE HOUSE OF MY GOD, I have of mine own proper good, of gold and silver, which I have given to the house of my God, over and above all that I have prepared for the holy house.**

We need to follow David's example and set our affection on the things of God. In this case, David set his affection, or his heart's desire, on the building of God's house — His temple.

David gathered the nation of Israel. He mobilized them for the purpose of building God's house. God wanted a temple, and David decided that he was going to be the one to start the process. So he told the nation: "I've taken all the gold, silver, and stones out of the national treasury and set them aside to build God's house. But besides that, I've taken things out of my own treasury because I want to build God's house."

There are two things I want you to notice about David: First, David was a blessed man. He took gold and silver from his own account as well as from the national account (v. 3), which means that he had it to give — he had a treasury.

Second, his heart was to do the things of God — in this case, to start building God's temple.

Let's continue reading in First Chronicles.

1 CHRONICLES 29:6-9
6 Then the chief of the fathers and princes of the tribes of Israel, and the captains of thousands and of hundreds, with the rulers of the king's work, offered willingly,
7 And gave for the service of the house of God of gold five thousand talents and ten thousand drams, and of silver ten thousand talents, and of brass eighteen thousand talents, and one hundred thousand talents of iron.
8 And they with whom precious stones were found gave them to the treasure of the house of the Lord, by the hand of Jehiel the Gershonite.
9 Then the people rejoiced, for that they offered willingly, because with perfect heart they offered willingly to the Lord: and David the king also rejoiced with great joy.

Notice what happened here. David set an example for the people. He set his affection on God's house, and then he acted on His love for God by *giving*.

One thing you have to learn about being a leader is that you must set the right example and the right tone for your ministry, organization, department, office, crew, home, and so forth if you want those under your leadership to submit to you and follow you. If you want your people to be on time, *you* have to be on time. If you want your people to serve the Lord, *you* have to serve the Lord. If you want them to be people of prayer, *you* have to be a person of prayer. And if you want them to give to the work of God, *you* have to be a giver.

Because David set the right example and gave, the people gave too. And the people not only gave, but they gave *willingly* and of a perfect heart. God looks at the heart, and the Bible says these people gave with the right motive.

When you give unto God, it's not good enough just to give. You have to give *with the right motive*. God looks on your heart just as much as He looks on your actions. You cannot give an offering and think, *God, I'm just giving this offering because I expect to get something back.* No, He wants you to give willingly and cheerfully because you love and believe in the work of God. First and foremost, that has to be your motive. *Then* you can believe God for a return, because He promised you one (Luke 6:38).

Did you know that you can do what is right in God's sight and still have the wrong heart about it? You have to make sure that what you're doing is what God wants you to do and that you're doing it out of a perfect heart — for the right reason, not for some other reason.

So God's purpose for David was for him to deliver Israel out of the hand of all their enemies and also to begin the building of the temple. But God's purpose didn't stop there. He didn't want a half-finished temple, and He didn't just want Israel to be delivered from all their enemies. *He wanted them to be so prosperous that their enemies would come running to them.* When David died, God needed another man to take His plans on to the next level.

Solomon Took to the Next Level What David Had Done

God had David *start* the temple, but He had Solomon *finish* the temple. In the following passage of Scripture, David shared some words of wisdom with his son, Solomon, before he died.

1 CHRONICLES 28:9
9 And thou, Solomon my son, know thou the God of thy father, and serve him with a perfect heart and with a willing mind: for the Lord searcheth all hearts, and understandeth all the imaginations of the thoughts: IF THOU SEEK HIM, HE WILL BE FOUND OF THEE; but if thou forsake him, he will cast thee off for ever.

David told Solomon to seek the Lord. If you're trying to get answers regarding God's will for your life, the Scripture says to seek God. If you will seek Him, you will find out His will for your life. This is the kind of thing David shared with his son.

Then we find God's purpose for Solomon in the next verse.

1 CHRONICLES 28:10
10 Take heed now; for the Lord hath chosen thee [Solomon] to build an house for the sanctuary: be strong, and do it.

David told Solomon that God had chosen him to finish building the temple. In the next chapter, we can read that Solomon indeed finished the temple, having picked up where his father left off.

Solomon Was an 'Evangelist'!

Now the Queen of Sheba came to Solomon when she heard about what the Lord had done for him. Let's read what she did.

1 KINGS 10:1-5
1 And when the queen of Sheba heard of the fame of Solomon concerning the name of the Lord, she came to prove him with hard questions.
2 And she came to Jerusalem with a very great train, with camels that bare spices, and very much gold, and precious

**stones: and when she was come to Solomon, she communed
with him of all that was in her heart.
3 And Solomon told her all her questions: there was not
any thing hid from the king, which he told her not.
4 And when the queen of Sheba had seen all Solomon's
wisdom, and the house that he had built,
5 And the meat of his table, and the sitting of his servants,
and the attendance of his ministers, and their apparel, and
his cupbearers, and his ascent by which he went up unto
the house of the Lord; there was no more spirit in her.**

The Queen of Sheba came to Solomon with riches as a
customary offering because she wanted to learn from him the
answers to her questions. We learn from this that the king of
Israel changed from fighting other nations as David had
done to welcoming other nations and introducing them to
God!

The Queen of Sheba not only had the chance to hear
Solomon's wisdom, but she also had the opportunity to see the
temple of God. She saw Solomon walk up to the house of the
Lord to worship Him. This great man who was so rich and
wise came reverently before God. He got on his knees to
worship the King of kings and Lord of lords, and she just
fainted at the sight of it all — she could hardly take it all in
(v. 5) ! (*See* also First Kings chapter 10 and Second Chronicles
chapter 9.)

David fought the wars and started the temple. Solomon
welcomed the world and finished the temple. Solomon took what
his father, David, had done to the next level.

Let me show you one other thing that Solomon did for the
nation of Israel.

1 KINGS 10:27
27 And the king made silver to be in Jerusalem as stones, and cedars made he to be as the sycomore trees that are in the vale, for abundance.

Solomon wasn't the only one who suddenly became prosperous — so prosperous, in fact, that the rest of the world couldn't help but notice it. Solomon caused the whole *nation* to be prosperous as well. During Solomon's time, silver became like stones. Can you imagine silver becoming that plentiful today and still retaining its value? You could just go outside, look down on the ground, and say, "Oh, look at all that silver." That's how rich Solomon made the nation of Israel.

Solomon picked up where David left off and took it to the next level. And that's God's will for this generation — to take the Church to the next level. That's talking about *you*!

Pick Up the Ball and Keep Running!

God's will for the Church as a whole is that it increase, grow spiritually, and reach more of the world for Jesus. But for that to happen, the Church has to keep going forward. It can't go through a rebuilding process every twenty or thirty years as a new generation is raised up.

Think about a winning football team whose star player retires. Then imagine that many of the team members get injured. Everything goes flat; they have to rebuild to even get to the place they were before, much less go higher. So then they get a star player, and after about five or ten years, they're able to get back to that same level of success again.

God doesn't have time for His Church to go through that process every time one generation gets old or dies. He expects every generation to pick up the ball and keep running with it, so to speak. He wants them to *continue* to fulfill His purpose.

Too many times, young people, especially PKs, are dropping the ball. We see it all the time. God uses a man to build a great ministry or business. Then the son comes in behind him and wrecks everything the father did. So everything God did through that family is ruined, and God then has to start over again with someone else who will do things His way.

God is calling this generation to take to another level what He has accomplished through past generations before us. He is calling us to do more for God than our fathers, our elders, did so that more of His plan and purpose can be accomplished in the *next* twenty years than was accomplished in the *last* twenty years. If we don't pick up the ball and keep running with it, the Church as a whole won't be able to increase.

I think that is what has happened over time. God raises up a generation and then the next generation drops the ball. So God has to do everything again to continue to build His Church. That's why we have so many revivals — because something has to be revived! That's not God's will. He doesn't want it to *revive*; He wants it to *continue*. He wants it to increase. He wants it to go to the next level.

Joshua Took to the Next Level What Moses Had Done

You are no doubt familiar with the story of Moses. God used him to deliver Israel out of Egypt. He was told to bring Israel to the Promised Land. But that generation never made it, because of unbelief and sin. But God's ultimate purpose for Israel was for them to be in the Promised Land.

Moses brought the Israelites out of Egypt with silver and gold; that was a great miracle. But God didn't want them living off miracles anymore. He wanted them living in the flow of blessings. And the blessings were in the Promised Land. So after Moses died, God raised up another young man by the name of Joshua.

Let's read what the Lord said to Joshua.

JOSHUA 1:1-5
1 Now after the death of Moses the servant of the Lord it came to pass, that the Lord spake unto Joshua the son of Nun, Moses' minister, saying,
2 Moses my servant is dead; now therefore arise, go over this Jordan, thou, and all this people, unto the land which I do give to them, even to the children of Israel.
3 Every place that the sole of your foot shall tread upon, that have I given unto you, as I said unto Moses.
4 From the wilderness and this Lebanon even unto the great river, the river Euphrates, all the land of the Hittites, and unto the great sea toward the going down of the sun, shall be your coast.
5 There shall not any man be able to stand before thee all the days of thy life: as I was with Moses, so I will be with thee: I will not fail thee, nor forsake thee.

Joshua did exactly what God wanted him to do. He took the Israelites into the Promised Land. Now God had used Moses to deliver the people from slavery and bondage. They had to be delivered from Egypt before they could even begin to walk in God's blessings. But then God used Joshua to take them further and put them in a place that was just plain blessed — the Promised Land!

Remember, in the days of Moses, the Israelites murmured and complained. They built gold idols out of the gold God had given them. They didn't in any way serve the Lord. But Joshua 24:31 says, *"And ISRAEL SERVED THE LORD ALL THE DAYS OF*

JOSHUA, and all the days of the elders that overlived Joshua, and which had known all the works of the Lord, that he had done for Israel."

What happened? God used Joshua to take what Moses had done to the next level.

I think you can see more clearly that God thinks in terms of generations and calls one generation to take to the next level what the previous generation accomplished.

The Disciples Took to the Next Level What Jesus Had Done

God wants this generation — a God-glorifying generation — to take His work to the next level. Jesus said, *"Verily, verily, I say unto you, He that believeth on me, THE WORKS THAT I DO SHALL HE DO ALSO; AND GREATER WORKS THAN THESE SHALL HE DO; because I go unto my Father"* (John 14:12).

Think about Jesus' words! All the works that Jesus did — including raising the dead and healing the sick — are to be done by the person who believes on Him. Do you believe on Jesus? Then He is talking about *you!*

The disciples believed on Jesus and took what He did to the next level. Acts 1:8 says, *"But ye shall receive power, after that the Holy Ghost is come upon you: and ye shall be witnesses unto me BOTH IN JERUSALEM, AND IN ALL JUDEA, AND IN SAMARIA, AND UNTO THE UTTERMOST PART OF THE EARTH."*

When Jesus ministered on earth, He only covered a couple of hundred miles, but how much territory did His disciples cover? Countless more miles than just a couple of hundred! In that way, the disciples took what Jesus did to the next level. Jesus reached a certain amount of people with the Gospel. But Jesus told the disciples to reach many more people with the Gospel, and they did.

If God's will for Elisha, Isaac, Joshua, Solomon, and the disciples was to take what was done by their spiritual leaders to the next level, don't you think the same is true for you and me today? God has great expectations for this generation! God has great expectations for *you*!

Chapter 2
God Has Plans for You!

Rev. Keith Butler II

God has a particular plan for this generation. He has not excluded us from His design to reap a harvest of souls from the earth and to consummate this Age, sending Jesus back for His Church. Instead, He has a purpose that He expects this generation to fulfill. And in this chapter, we are going to find out what God's plan is for this generation.

In the last chapter, I talked about one generation taking to the next level the work accomplished by the previous generation. But in order for a generation as a whole to take what has already been done to another level, *individuals* must do their part. Not only does God want us as a generation to go further and higher than the generation before us, He wants us *individually* to go further and higher.

Each of Us Must Answer
The Call and Rise to the Task

It's difficult for a team of any kind to be successful if the individual team members aren't successful. In other words, a team can't be called skilled and talented if individual team members aren't skilled and talented. So for God to cause this generation to do more than those before them, each one individually must allow God to do in him or her whatever He needs to do. We must take our place in a God-glorifying generation!

In First Corinthians 12:12, the Body of Christ is likened to the human body. Just as in the human body, if one part or member of the Body of Christ isn't functioning properly, the whole Body suffers. That's why it's so important that each of us finds his place and takes it — so we can continually move forward and continue the work of God, taking it to the next level.

Don't 'Kick Against the Pricks'

Each person in the Body of Christ should play a part in reaching the world with the Gospel of the Lord Jesus Christ. In fact, in order for the whole Body of Christ to be successful in accomplishing God's plan and purpose, every one in the Body — every different part — must do his or her job.

Let's read about the Apostle Paul to find out what his specific job was in reaching the world with the Gospel.

> **ACTS 26:13,14**
> **13 At midday, O king, I saw in the way a light from heaven, above the brightness of the sun, shining round about me and them which journeyed with me.**
> **14 And when we were all fallen to the earth, I heard a voice speaking unto me, and saying in the Hebrew tongue, Saul, Saul, why persecutest thou me? it is hard for thee to kick against the pricks.**

Paul, who was still Saul at the time, and his company were traveling the road to Damascus when a light shone brightly around him. The light was so great that it was brighter than the sun (v. 13). It was the glory of the Lord, and the Bible says that everyone in Paul's company fell to the ground.

Sometimes when a man or woman of God lays hands on the sick, the sick who are being ministered to fall down. The reason for that is when the power of God comes in contact with human flesh, something has to give, and it's not going to be the power of God! That's what happened on the road to Damascus. Paul and his company couldn't even stand up because of the power of God.

Remember, these men were not believers at the time. These men were on their way to Damascus to get Christians and throw them into jail. But when the glory of God showed up, they hit the ground!

Paul said that he heard a Voice. And Paul related that the Voice spoke to him in his native language, the Hebrew tongue. God didn't come to Paul in the English tongue or in the Greek tongue. God spoke to him in his own language.

God knows your language. God knows how to talk to you. In other words, He knows how to get across to you what you need to know. He knows what to say in a way that you can understand. So don't be concerned about hearing from God. If you seek Him, God will tell you what you need to know.

Notice what God said to Paul: "... *it is hard for thee to kick against the pricks*" (v. 14). What did God mean? God was saying, "You're going against what I have planned for your life. You're going against My will. And your life is hard because you're trying to kick against the pricks."

You may understand firsthand the situation Paul was in, because you may be "kicking against the pricks" in your own life. God has a plan for your life. (And you may already know God's plan for your life; it may not be a mystery to you.) You may know what God wants you to do, but you may not want to do it. You may be trying to do things your way rather than God's way. And that's why your life is getting harder and harder.

You see, since God has a plan for your life, if you're making the decision to do things your own way, what you are telling God is, "You are not equipped to be my God. *I* am my God, and I will choose what I do, when to do it, how to do it, and where to do it."

God Appeared to Paul for a Purpose (God Had a Plan!)

Let's continue reading about Paul's experience on the road to Damascus.

> **ACTS 26:15-18**
> **15 And I said, Who art thou, Lord? And he said, I am Jesus whom thou persecutest.**
> **16 But rise, and stand upon thy feet: for I HAVE APPEARED UNTO THEE FOR THIS PURPOSE, TO MAKE THEE A MINISTER AND A WITNESS both of these things which thou hast seen, and of those things in the which I will appear unto thee;**
> **17 Delivering thee from the people, AND FROM THE GENTILES, UNTO WHOM NOW I SEND THEE,**
> **18 TO OPEN THEIR EYES, AND TO TURN THEM FROM DARKNESS TO LIGHT, AND FROM THE POWER OF SATAN UNTO GOD, that they may receive forgiveness of sins, and inheritance among them which are sanctified by faith that is in me.**

God told Paul that He had appeared to him for this purpose: to *make* him (v. 16), to *deliver* him (v. 17), to *send* him (v. 17), and to *work with* him (v. 18). God showed up to *make* Paul a minister and a witness. God showed up to *deliver* Paul from the people. God showed up to *send* Paul to the people. And, finally, God told Paul that He would *work with him*, accomplishing His wonders through Paul's life.

Paul couldn't have opened anybody's spiritual eyes on his own. The Holy Ghost is the revealer of truth. He is the One who opens the eyes of the lost and allows them to see Jesus as He is. But even then, that couldn't have happened in Paul's life unless Paul preached. God called Paul so that He could work with him to get people saved and discipled so they could walk in their inheritance in Christ.

At the time God appeared to Paul, Paul was a spiritual criminal. He was out to get believers and put them in jail. He wanted to see them die because of whom they believed in. Paul didn't believe in Jesus at the time. But God showed up and began to talk to Paul about His plan for his future, and Paul became a believer.

Acts 9:15 and 16 says, *"But the Lord said unto him* [Ananias, whom God had commanded to go minister to Paul], *Go thy way: for he* [Paul] *is a chosen vessel unto me, to bear my name BEFORE THE GENTILES, AND KINGS, AND THE CHILDREN OF ISRAEL: For I will shew him how great things he must suffer for my name's sake."*

In this passage of Scripture, God spoke to Ananias about His plan for Paul's future. God summed up Paul's entire life in one sentence: "He's a chosen vessel who will bear My Name before the Gentiles." And we know that Paul's ministry was primarily to the Gentiles. Every time Paul went to a new town, he spoke to the Israelites first. Once they rejected him, he went to the Gentiles. Paul was also brought before kings, where he testified about Jesus.

The final thing God told Ananias about Paul's future was that he would suffer many things for the Lord (Acts 9:16). And we know that Paul did that too.

God had a particular plan designed for Paul to follow so that he could end up being one of the greatest men ever on the face of the earth. God had a plan for Paul, and since God had a plan for Paul, we know that God has a plan for you!

God Had a Plan for Peter

Remember in the Bible that Peter told Jesus that he would not forsake Him but would go with Him even to the grave. But Jesus said, "No, before the cock crows, you will deny me three times" (Luke 22:60,61).

Now when Jesus was brought before the rulers just before His crucifixion, Peter had three opportunities to let them know that he was with Jesus. But every time, he chose instead to deny Him. And then the Bible says, "The cock crew and Jesus looked at him" (Luke 22:60,61). Can you imagine how Peter must have felt as what Jesus predicted came to pass? He ran out and wept bitterly.

Let's read in John chapter 21 to find out what Peter decided to do after Jesus was crucified.

> **JOHN 21:3**
> **3 Simon Peter saith unto them, I go a fishing. They say unto him, We also go with thee. They went forth, and entered into a ship immediately; and that night they caught nothing.**

Peter was a fisherman before Jesus came into his life. Fishing was what he was successful at. So when the time came when he felt he had failed Jesus, he gave up as an apostle and went back to his old life of fishing. And because Peter was the leader, others said, "I'm going with you, Peter." And they followed him. But this verse says that they entered a ship and caught nothing all night.

When Jesus came back to the earth, He looked for Peter. He wanted to restore him. Let's read what Jesus said.

JOHN 21:15-17
15 So when they had dined, Jesus saith to Simon Peter, Simon, son of Jonas, LOVEST THOU ME MORE THAN THESE? He saith unto him, Yea, Lord; thou knowest that I love thee. He saith unto him, Feed my lambs.
16 He saith to him again the second time, Simon, son of Jonas, LOVEST THOU ME? He saith unto him, Yea, Lord; thou knowest that I love thee. He saith unto him, Feed my sheep.
17 He saith unto him the third time, Simon, son of Jonas, LOVEST THOU ME? Peter was grieved because he said unto him the third time, Lovest thou me? And he said unto him, Lord, thou knowest all things; thou knowest that I love thee. Jesus saith unto him, Feed my sheep.

Notice what Jesus was asking him: "Do you love Me more than these fish? Do you love Me more than this money? Do you love Me more than the security of knowing that if you live your life this way, you'll have a certain amount of money? Jesus gave him three opportunities to tell Him that he loved Him. Remember Peter failed three times. Jesus gave him the opportunity to *succeed* three times!

Then Jesus gave Peter a glimpse of his future.

JOHN 21:18,19
18 Verily, verily, I say unto thee, When thou wast young, thou girdest thyself, and walkedst whither thou wouldest: but when thou shalt be old, thou shalt stretch forth thy hands, and another shall gird thee, and carry thee whither thou wouldest not.
19 This spake he, signifying by what death he should glorify God. And when he had spoken this, he saith unto him, Follow me.

In essence, Jesus told Peter, "When you were young, this is what happened. And when you get old, this is what's going to happen." Jesus even gave Peter a glimpse of the way that Peter would die. Jesus knew then what was going to happen in Peter's life.

Notice that Jesus took the time to sit down with Peter before He went back to Heaven. He had to give Peter the opportunity to be restored and to know that he was forgiven. At a fish dinner, Jesus took the time to bring Peter back to God, because God had a plan for Peter.

God saw the plan He had for Peter. He saw Peter on the Day of Pentecost preaching and getting 3,000 people saved. God saw Peter as a leader of the Early Church. God saw Peter as the first one to go to the Gentiles. God saw Peter doing all these great things. God saw Peter as blessed. So Jesus thought, *God has a plan for Peter, so let me sit down and make sure Peter is okay. I want Peter to follow and fulfill God's plan.*

Have you ever messed up before? Has God ever taken the time to get you restored to Him? Of course, He has. God takes the time to work with us. And the Holy Spirit talks to us and comforts us, showing us that everything is going to be okay. God shows us that our sin was washed away and thrown into the sea of forgetfulness (Micah 7:19).

Why would He do this for you? Because God has plans for you!

Listen to God, Not to People

Genesis 12:1 says, *"Now the Lord had said unto Abram, Get thee out of thy country, and from thy kindred, and from thy father's house, unto a land that I will shew thee."* God told Abraham to get away from his country and from his father's house, his neighborhood, his crazy cousins, and so on! In the previous verse, we learn that Abraham's father died. Abraham knew before his father died that God wanted him to leave, but he didn't do it (*see* Genesis chapter 11). He waited until after his father died.

God told Abraham to get away from certain people. God didn't have anything against those people; He just wanted Abraham to obey Him and to follow His plan, not his own plan or his family's. God has a plan for your life, too, but you will not be successful if you let people tell you what God's will is for your life.

If you continue to let people — whether it is your mother, father, other family members, or close friends — tell you that what God has spoken to you is not His will, you are tying God's hands, so to speak. God cannot fulfill His plan for you because you won't obey Him and walk in it. You shouldn't pay any attention to those who come against what you know God has told you.

Also, don't let unbelievers tell you what to do. They don't know anything about spiritual things, and their actions prove it. For example, why would you smoke a cigarette if you knew that it would cause you to stink, have bad breath, harm your health, and possibly make you miserably sick or kill you? Why would you have sex outside of marriage if you knew that you could get some kind of incurable and, possibly, terminal disease?

Why would you run in and out of clubs all the time if you knew that you could end up in a fight and be killed? The world does it all the time. Why? They are blind. They can't see God's plan. They don't see the value in refraining from those things, because they don't have a clear vision for their future.

Don't let those who are spiritually blind lead you in life. They will lead you into a ditch! Don't pay any attention to them. You're of a different Kingdom. You are a holy nation, a peculiar people, a chosen generation, and a royal priesthood (1 Peter 2:9)! You're here on this earth to get those people saved, not to heed their counsel and follow their ungodly example.

God Had a Plan for Abraham

In Genesis 12:2 and 3, God said to Abraham, *"And I will make of thee a great nation, and I WILL BLESS THEE, and make thy name great; and thou shalt be a blessing: And I will bless them that bless thee, and curse him that curseth thee: and in thee shall all families of the earth be blessed."* God told Abraham that He would personally bless him.

Now the word "blessed" means *empowered to prosper* or *anointed to prosper*. God will anoint you so that anybody who comes and blesses you will also be blessed. That anointing upon you will rub off on them. And when you're in God's perfect will, God will curse anybody who curses you.

God told Abraham, "In you will all the families of the earth be blessed." How could all the families of the earth be blessed in Abraham, naturally speaking? God had to be talking about something else here — something that was in Abraham that would bless the whole planet forever. What was it? It was his *seed*.

Think back for a minute. Where did Jesus come from regarding human lineage? Jesus was of the seed of Abraham. When God first called Abraham, God was making mention of Jesus! When God said that all the families of the earth would be blessed through Abraham, He was referring to Abraham's seed; He was referring to Jesus!

God had a plan for Abraham that caused him to be the ancestor of Jesus. The day God called him, God had a plan for Abraham's entire life. God planned for him to be so rich, so blessed, and so great that to this day would we talk about

Abraham and the fact that Jesus was his descendant. And we know that since God had a plan for Abraham from the very beginning, God has a plan for *you*!

Is It a Good Idea or a *'God'* Idea

God stated His plan for Abraham in Genesis 12:1 — to get out of the land he was in and go to a land God would show him. Abraham didn't just wake up one day and say, "I have an idea; I'll go find a new land. Well, I guess I should leave." No, God told him to leave everybody and go to a land He would show him. That was *God's* idea, not Abraham's.

There's a difference between just a *good* idea and a *"God* idea."* A good idea is just that — a good idea. And when you choose a good idea over a "God idea," you choose to live life based on your ability rather than on God's ability. If you do that, you will never reach your full potential in life or feel completely satisfied.

For example, you may want to be a chemical engineer because you know that chemical engineers make a lot of money. But if God has called you to be a minister, you'd better follow Him. And it's nice to be a doctor, but not if God has called you to be a lawyer! It's nice to be an athlete, but not if God has called you to be a doctor. God's way is the best way; it will always lead you to success and fulfillment in life beyond your wildest dreams.

You need to know what God wants you to do in life, because when you follow God's *plan*, you end up in God's *land*. God's land where your life is concerned is that place where He wants you to be. It's His perfect will for you. And there's more than enough in God's land. There's health, peace, joy, and happiness in God's land.

So God told Abraham to leave everybody and go to a land that He had for him. Notice that God did not tell Abraham where the land was.

You may not know exactly where you're going. But all you need to know is to follow God, trust Him, and stay with Him and His plan as He leads you step by step. You may not know about even the next step, but you can make the decision to do whatever He says simply because He says it.

I can talk about this firsthand. My own plan as young man just out of high school was to go to business school and eventually make lots of money. I had received a full scholarship to a university that doesn't give too many full rides to their school. But I was going. I had everything planned. I knew where I was going to live while I was in school. I even had friends there in that town. Then God said, "Forget your scholarship and go to RHEMA Bible Training Center in Broken Arrow, Oklahoma."

People thought I was a fool for passing up such a huge scholarship and going to a Bible school where the credits I earned would never benefit me in a secular school. I had the opportunity to really be blessed at the university; the way was paved before me. But it wasn't *God's* idea. It was just a *good* idea. So I did what God said, and things have worked out tremendously for me as a result.

Now things didn't work out like that overnight. In fact, there were times things didn't seem to be working out at all. But even when things look bad and nothing seems to be working out, the very best thing you can do is to continue following God's plan for your life, doing what He wants you to do.

Missteps in Dating:
When God's Plans Meet Satan's Pitfalls

Following God to achieve His highest and best applies not only to your vocation and calling in life; it also applies to relationships, dating, and marriage.

For example, as a young single female, your mind may say, *I've got a pretty good man. He goes to college. He's pretty nice to me most of the time. Since this is the best guy I've been around in a while, I'm going to stay with him, at least for now. I don't want to be alone.*

In other words, single woman, the man you're with may not meet all the criteria on your "list," but he seems good enough at the time to get involved with, and you sort of forget what you were believing God for in a mate. You lose sight of your future and the mate God has for you in order to gratify yourself "here and now."

Single person, you need to check up on what God said to you. Did God say to date that person? Did God say to even hang out with him or her? Do you have a check in your spirit that you shouldn't be with that person? Don't wait until you're emotionally involved with someone to obey what God is telling you.

You don't *need* a boyfriend. You don't *need* a girlfriend. The devil knows that there are certain things planned for your future, so as you're running your race, he sends pitfalls across your path to try to trip you up. And that pitfall sometimes comes in the form of a particular man or woman.

In the Book of Proverbs, the Bible refers to the "strange woman." She is out to get you. She knows where you are, and she follows you around. The minute you stop seeking God and start seeking something else, she'll be right there to meet you. The

Bible says that it's not her *hips* that entice you to be with her; it's her *lips*. In other words, she knows how to talk to you. You may think you've met the finest woman in the world because of the way she treats you. But her ways lead to death (Prov. 2:10-19; *see* Proverbs chapter 7).

In every area of life, you have to make the decision, "Am I going to follow *my* plan, my good idea, or *God's* plan?"

Are you in this thing for real? Are you going to live your life to glorify God? Are you going to trust God that He has a good plan for your life? These are questions you're going to have to answer if you're going to walk in God's best blessings and avoid the devil's pitfalls.

Choose Life — Choose God's Way!

The world's way of doing things is like a travel brochure. It entices you by showing you a picture of how things will be when you follow its directions. Where you're going may look pretty, but when you get to your destination, you'll find out that it doesn't offer all the things you thought it would.

Let me give you a natural illustration. When I was growing up, my family went on a vacation to a place my mother found in a travel brochure called Jekyll Island. We received all kinds of information about the island, including the place where we would be staying and the activities on the island. All the pictures we receive showed a very beautiful, inviting place. The brochures said that we would have a great time.

But when we actually got to Jekyll Island, we lasted only half a day! The place where we were supposed to stay was a dump! That colorful brochure never showed us all the roaches that were there in that room! And life was boring on that island. The brochure showed us a swimming pool, but never told us that it wasn't maintained very well and that it even contained "wildlife" — a large, cranky crab that tried to claw us! We ended up calling it "Jerk Island."

That's how the world is. They try to tell you that your life will be better if you go their way. But when you "get there," it's horrible.

Some people say, "I've been in church and have served God all my life. I've done good things for God. But I just want to see what's out there. I've never seen what's out there in the world." Leave it alone! You may not get back. Stay with God. There's nothing out there for you. God's plan and His land are better!

God Makes Dreamers

God has placed divine dreams in your heart. And if you know anything about a divine dream — a dream given by God — it is usually something that seems far-fetched or ridiculous in the natural.

God has a dream of a born-again, Spirit-filled, Word-talking, faith-walking man of God being the President of the United States. God has a dream of the richest man who runs the most powerful company on the planet being a man who understands the principles of living to be a blessing instead of living for more greedy gain.

God has a dream of the greatest movie that breaks all box-office records to be one that glorifies the King of kings and the Lord of lords! God has a dream of churches that are full of 100,000 people rather than 100 people. God has a dream of millions of people coming together on a Friday night — not to watch a basketball game — but to pray before God.

God has a dream of doing all these great things. So what does He do? He takes different pieces of His dream and puts a piece in you. He takes another piece and puts it in someone else. He can make one person a great movie producer. He can make another the world's richest man or woman. And He can make someone who's following Him the President of the United States.

The dream God has placed in you may not make sense. But if it's God's dream, God will perform it. He will bring it to pass! God will never tell you to do something you do cannot do. You may not have the ability in yourself, but, in Him, you have the ability to fulfill that dream!

Yes, it may seem like a ridiculous dream if you're thinking about doing it in your own ability. But God is not telling you to do it in your own ability; God is talking about taking His "super-" and adding it to your "natural" so that you can do the supernatural here on planet Earth!

And for that dream to happen, all you have to do is stay with God's plan. God has a plan for you, so find out what that plan is and fulfill your role in this generation. Glorify God and help win the world to Jesus by doing your part.

When God created the earth, He had a picture on the inside of Him of what He was going to create before He ever spoke it into existence. Now God has placed a picture inside of you, a picture from Him of what your life can and should be. And He wants you to go ahead and make it happen as you follow Him. But you have to stay with His plan.

Don't be an average "Joe Christian" who is sick one day and not sick the next day. Instead, walk in divine health. Don't be someone who is in and out of debt. Instead, learn about a budget and walk in divine prosperity. Remember, God adds His "super-" to your "natural." That means you still have to do natural things. You still have to go to work or school. You still have to do the things you're supposed to do. But don't be average. Be successful in your ability, but let the Holy Ghost take you to the next level.

God makes dreamers. There's nothing wrong with being a dreamer. And it doesn't matter where you come from or what color your skin is, you can fulfill your dream. People can't tell me that because I'm a black man, I can't be successful. That's foolishness; it's worldly. That's their way of thinking, but it's not true.

Take the limits off your mind. Take the limits off your heart. *God is limitless!* The only way He is limited is if you limit Him. Make a decision to go with God's plan and stay with His plan no matter what, for if you do, you are guaranteed from the Word of God that your life will get better and brighter every step of the way!

You are a part of the greatest period of mankind that ever was. The glory of God is being manifested more and more at the same time judgment is approaching. God is doing more by His Spirit now than He's ever done, and He's only building up to the big day when He's going to bring everyone home who's called on the Name of Jesus Christ as Savior. This is the generation God has chosen to usher in that day!

You Are on God's Mind

We are the generation that will see Jesus return. We are the generation that will cause the world to say, "Wow! God is real!" That means that God has a plan for you to do something that may seem impossible.

Jeremiah 29:11 says, *"For I know the thoughts that I think toward you, saith the Lord, thoughts of peace, and not of evil, to give you an expected end."* The word "thoughts" also means *plans.* God knows the plans that He has for you. God has you on His mind. He is thinking about you. God has thoughts of peace for you. God is not out to stop you or to hurt you. No! One translation says, "God will give you the end that you long for." God wants you to have a life that you couldn't even dream of!

In the Book of Proverbs, we are given a clear picture of what our future looks like.

> **PROVERBS 4:18 (*Amplified*)**
> **18 But the path of the** [uncompromisingly] **just and righteous is like the light of dawn, that shines MORE AND MORE** (BRIGHTER and clearer) **until** [it reaches its full strength and glory in] **the perfect day [to be prepared].**

As long as you stay on His path, this what God is telling you about your future Every day that you walk on His path may not be easy. Every day that you walk on His path may not be the most fun. But when you look back, you'll find that your path got brighter and brighter as you went along.

Then, if you're single, God brings someone special into your life — someone you've been believing for — and your path gets even brighter. Then you get the dream house you've had in your heart for many years, and your path gets brighter still. Then your business or ministry becomes successful and you go up to the next level; your life just got a little brighter. Financially, you enjoyed a good status, but then God gives you a boost and your status changes; you become a multi-millionaire. Your life just got a lot brighter!

You see, you are guaranteed that your life will get better and better as you walk on this earth in God's perfect will. The world cannot guarantee that kind of success if you go its way instead of God's way. But walking in God's way, you will reach a point where you'll say, "Wow! God is good today." Then tomorrow you'll say, "God is better today." And the next day, you'll say, "Whoa! God is showing up now!"

And the rest of your life, you will be saying, "God is awesome!" Why? Because God has a plan for you. Your path is a guaranteed path that leads to glory. And you get a little piece of glory every single step of the way.

God has designed you to fulfill a particular part of His plan. You are part of a team. You are part of this generation that God has raised up. And you won't be happy until you do what you're designed to do. But if you do what you're designed to do, you'll find much fulfillment and happiness.

Chapter 3
No Vision — No Future

Minister MiChelle Butler

Have you ever filled out a job application or gone for an interview in which you were asked, "Where do you see yourself in ten years?" Why would employers ask you that? Because they understand the importance of vision. They understand that a person of vision has a future.

Now if you answer their question by saying, "I see myself as one of the executives in this corporation," they will see you as a person with vision! The employer realizes that if you are planning to become a top executive in the corporation, you will come to work on time and do your very best.

But if you answer the question by saying, "I'm just looking for a job right now. I need some money, and this seems like a good opportunity. So here I am," they will be hesitant to hire you. You have no vision. The minute another job comes along that pays better money, they know you will leave.

What Is Vision?

Proverbs 29:18 says, *"Where there is no vision, the people perish: but he that keepeth the law, happy is he."* This scripture is saying the same thing that any good employer knows: a person with a vision is going to direct his or her life according to that vision.

For example, a guy in high school says that he wants to be a lawyer. You can be sure that if he is really serious, he will be concentrating on getting good grades. Why? Because he understands that if he wants to be a lawyer in the future, he has to get good grades now so he can get into a good college. Then when he gets into college, he has to get good grades there so that he can get into a good law school.

The temptation in high school is to just "kill it" on the grades. Many students just want to graduate, so they slide by, doing as little as they can get away with — just enough to make it. And the temptation is even greater to just party all the time. But a person with a vision of being a lawyer will choose to study rather than party. He will align himself and his behavior with his vision.

As born-again, Spirit-filled believers, where should our vision come from? Everybody has a call of God on his or her life. You may not be called to the pulpit ministry, but that doesn't mean you don't have a calling. God does not make mistakes and He does not waste faith. You are not an accident, no matter what circumstance you were born under. God has a specific purpose and will for you on this earth. There is a reason you are here.

So where should your vision come from? Does it come from outside influences or from the Spirit of God dealing with your spirit? For example, I love to watch the television show "Rescue 911." Does that mean that I'm called to be a paramedic? I also like the television show "Law and Order." Does that mean I'm supposed to be a cop? I also hear Pastor Butler preach, and I really love his church and the atmosphere there, so I must be a pastor, right? No. That's what the world says. They say, "Do whatever you feel like doing."

Your vision — the perfect will of God for your life — is found in God. When I looked up the word "vision," I found that it means *an image created in the imagination; a picture of your future; your goals, your dreams, those things you desire to attain.* If vision is a picture of my future, then let's define future. It is *the time yet to come.* Our vision of what God has planned for our future can come only from Him.

How Did Abraham Get His Vision?

When you think about Abraham, what do you think was his main aspiration in life? He had a vision to be the father of many nations. Where did he get that vision? Did he just wake up one day and decide he was going to be the father of many nations?

Let's read the account in Genesis that explains how Abraham got his vision.

> **GENESIS 15:2-6**
> **2 AND ABRAM SAID, Lord God, what wilt thou give me, seeing I go childless, and the steward of my house is this Eliezer of Damascus?**
> **3 And Abram said, Behold, to me thou hast given no seed: and, lo, one born in my house is mine heir.**
> **4 AND, BEHOLD, THE WORD OF THE LORD CAME UNTO HIM, SAYING, This shall not be thine heir; but he that shall come forth out of thine own bowels shall be thine heir.**
> **5 And he brought him forth abroad, and said, Look now toward heaven, and tell the stars, if thou be able to number them: and he said unto him, So shall thy seed be.**
> **6 And he believed in the Lord; and he counted it to him for righteousness.**

Verse 2 says, *"And Abram said...."* Then verse 4 says, "And the word of the Lord came unto him." Notice that Abraham and the Lord are in a conversation. First, *Abraham* said, and then *God* said. Obviously, Abraham had to go to God and talk to Him long enough to hear the word of the Lord that came unto him.

Abraham was conversing with God; he was praying. Well, if Abraham found out the perfect will of God for his life through communication and prayer, then you can find out the will of God for *your* life through prayer.

Matthew 7:7 says, *"Ask, and it shall be given you; seek, and ye shall find; knock, and it shall be opened unto you."* If you do not know what the perfect will of God is for your life, ask and seek God. Spend time communicating with Him. That's what prayer is. In essence, it's communing with God.

Notice what Genesis 15:5 says: "Look now toward Heaven and tell the stars if you're able to number them." There are many stars in the sky. If you've ever gone outside on a clear night and looked up at the stars, you've seen plenty of them. Well, God said to Abraham, "So shall thy seed be." Abraham believed what the Lord said to him, and he was declared righteous (v. 6).

You have to believe God in order to benefit from His blessings. Abraham believed God. Now Abraham was not some nineteen-year-old with an eighteen-year-old wife, able to have many babies. No, he was old. And that was just one barrier. The other barrier was that his wife was barren. She couldn't have children regardless of her old age. God told Abraham something that seemed impossible in the natural. I mean, how could he become the father of many nations?

But Abraham trusted God. He knew something about the Lord. He knew that God is El Shaddai and that He is the covenant-keeping God. Once God says something, it is forever settled in Heaven. When God's Word is spoken, His power is available to change the circumstance. He knew that about the Lord through *relationship.*

When You Know God,
You Will Be Able To Trust Him

You have to trust someone in order to believe what he says. And you have to know that someone in order to trust him.

Let me give you an example. After graduating from RHEMA Bible Training Center, I decided to go back to the University of Michigan. I needed $2,000 in order to make the first payment on my tuition. I went to my mother and said, "Mom, I have a tuition payment due for $2,000."

She said, "Okay, let me get my checkbook and write you out a check for $2,000." You see, I know my mom. I know she has the money and that her check was good. Just because someone is dressed up in church and has jewelry on doesn't mean he or she has money. You have to know something about the person. I had to know something about my mom to not only know that she had the money, but that she had the money in the bank available to give to me!

When I was at RHEMA Bible Training Center, I had to take a class on finances. One thing they told us is that sometimes people write "faith checks" — these people don't have the money in the bank, but they believe that between the time they sign the check and the check is cashed, the money will somehow appear in their account.

If a stranger came to me and said, "I want to write a check for your tuition and make it payable to the University of Michigan," I would be very happy, but I would also call up the bank to make sure that money was there before I presented the check to the university. Why? Because that person is a stranger to me; I don't know him very well. It doesn't mean that anything is wrong with him. He could be the best person in the world, but if I don't know him, I'm going to have to call the bank to make sure he has the money on hand to make that check good!

You will have to trust God, not only to give you vision — dreams and goals of what your life can be — but to cause that vision to come to pass.

Your Vision Should Line Up
With the Word of God

People often associate positive circumstances with being in the perfect will of God. But the Word of God, not circumstances, must be your indicator. In other words, just because things may be going well in your life doesn't mean that you are in the perfect will of God. You have to get into the Word to determine God's will for your life and whether or not you are following His will.

God's Word is God speaking to you, and it will guide you in every area of life. Joshua 1:8 says, *"This book of the law shall not depart out of thy mouth; but thou shalt meditate therein day and night, that thou mayest observe to do according to all that is written therein: for then thou shalt make thy way prosperous, and then thou shalt have good success."*

The Word of God should be your "elimination standard." If something you're doing or want to do doesn't line up with the Word, automatically eliminate it. For example, God is not calling you to be an abortion clinic doctor who kills babies. That vision doesn't line up with the Word.

Think about a single woman or a single man. They have elimination standards. They don't go out with everybody who asks them. What are some of the things that will cause a godly woman to say, "No, I won't go out with you"? Well, if the man was unsaved or had no money, those things would probably cause a woman to "eliminate" him in terms of a relationship with him.

In the same way, a man will eliminate a girl if she gossips about other people or if she yells at people in anger. Everybody has an elimination standard. So if your vision isn't based on the Word, eliminate it.

The First Step to Finding God's Will: Abandon Your Own Will

To find out the will of God for your life, there are three steps that you can follow. *First*, abandon your own will. You have to realize that what you want no longer matters.

After high school, I went to the University of Michigan without even bothering to ask God what He wanted me to do. I had never asked God what His perfect will was for my life! Then my dad challenged me. He said, "Why don't you spend thirty minutes in prayer just strictly praying in tongues about what God's perfect will is for your life?"

I said, "Sure, okay." To be honest, I didn't expect God to tell me, "I never told you to go to the University of Michigan." But He did! Then He told me that I was supposed to be somewhere else. Now it was not what I wanted to hear. God said, "I didn't tell you to go to the University of Michigan; I called you to go to RHEMA. I called you to the ministry."

I did not want to go into the ministry at all. My father is in the ministry. My mother is in the ministry. My brother is in the ministry. That is enough. It doesn't take the whole family. I had decided a long time ago when I was just a kid that I wanted to go to college. But I had to abandon my own will. I had to know that God was on my side. I had to know that the calling on my life was not just for me, but it was for others too. I had to know that God had my best interest at heart. I had to trust Him. And I could do that, because I know Him.

The Second Step to Finding God's Will:
Get Free From People Who Would Hinder You

The *second* step in finding out the will of God for your life is to get free from people who would hinder you. When I finally accepted the call of God on my life to the full-time ministry, I called RHEMA and requested an application. Well, some of the first things I heard from people was, "You're going to RHEMA? Is your dad making you go? Is he going to send the whole family? Why don't you finish college first? You're going to be broke for the rest of your life."

I heard all kinds of things from people, but I had to get free from that. I had to have my relationship with God intact so I could know that He had a perfect plan for my life and follow it with confidence.

You have to get free from what people think. There is a call on your life. There is a purpose for your life, and people will try to stop you from fulfilling it. But it's not other people's job to understand the call of God on your life. Actually, it's none of their business.

When I returned home from RHEMA after two years and preached my first message, people came up to me after the service and said, "That was so anointed." I was thinking, *Lord, I'm so glad I listened to You. This is so great!*

Well, a few months later, I received my first "unfriendly" letter. It was addressed to me, but it was concerning both my brother and me. The letter said, "Can't you think for yourself? You sound too much like your dad. I've enclosed a list of Bible questions. See if you can answer them for yourself without any help from Dad." It was a very nasty letter.

Now I knew that letters like that would come, but it still shocked me. This was one of the reasons why I didn't want to go into the ministry. I could have just stopped there and allowed myself to become discouraged. But I knew there was a call on my life. And I knew that if I obeyed God, somebody would get saved and somebody would be filled with the Spirit. I had to get free from people — from their opinions of me.

The Third Step to Finding God's Will: Make a Firm Decision Not To Turn Back!

The *third* step in finding and fulfilling the will of God for your life is to make a firm decision not to turn back. Nobody said that life was fair. There will always be a reason to quit. There will always be somebody with a good point as to why you can't do what you're called to do.

When you're teaching a child how to ride a bike, he may peddle twice and fall off the bike. But you say, "Good job! You made it a whole foot!" You praise the child. And then when the child makes it to the end of the block, you praise him. But if you see a twenty- or thirty-year-old person fall off his bike, you might not say anything encouraging, perhaps because you don't think he should have fallen.

There will come a time when you won't have people patting you on the back. When you first start a job, people will usually encourage and help you. But after a while when you are doing the job better than you were at the beginning, there won't be anyone patting you on the back. You may think, *Where did everyone go?*

The devil will put the thought in your head, *Nobody knows the trouble I see.* And maybe nobody does understand what you're going through, but you have to make a firm decision not to turn around and go back.

You Will Have To Give an Account
To God for the Call on Your Life

When you abandon your own will, get free from people who would hinder you, and make a firm decision to never turn back, you will be free to obey God when He tells you to do something. You will have cultivated a relationship between you and Him. You know that He is El Shaddai, God Almighty, your Creator, your Bright and Morning Star, the Beginning and the End. And you will follow God because you're on a mission. You know that God placed you on this earth to fulfill His plan for your life. You have a vision and a future, and you will not allow yourself to be turned aside from fulfilling it.

Romans 11:29 says, *"For the gifts and calling of God are without repentance."* Whether you do what God has called you to do or not, you're still going to have to give an account to God for your calling — for what you did with it. God's calling does not go away just because you decide not to obey it. You will still have to give an account to God for the calling that is on your life.

Some people would like to obey God, but they feel they've disobeyed Him in the past so much that they'll never get back on track. One of the tricks of the enemy is to get you to think that you've messed up so bad that God can't use you. Many people think they are damaged goods, so to speak, and that God could never use them or anoint them to do anything. But Romans 11:29 says that the gifts and calling of God are without repentance.

God Still Used David After He Made a Mistake

King David is an example of someone who messed up big time and was still used of God after he repented. King David was the king, anointed by the Most High God. But he saw Bathsheba bathing on the roof one day and didn't turn away from the temptation. He looked at her and began to lust after her. He ended up sleeping with her, although she was married and her husband served David.

Later, David found out that Bathsheba was pregnant with his baby. So he had her husband killed and gave her two days to mourn. Then she moved into David's kingdom and became one of his wives.

Many of us think that God could never use a man like that. We are wrong! David repented of his sin (1 John 1:9) and God used David to, among other things, write many of the Psalms in the Bible. People have been reading the Book of Psalms for years. Burdens have been removed and yokes have been destroyed while reading the Psalms.

You may still be hung up on things you did before you were saved. Let that go, because the gifts and callings of God are without repentance. You're going to have to give an account for what God has called you to do. When you get to the throne of Heaven and you walk in there, you want God to say to you, "Well done, my good and faithful servant." So purpose in your heart to seek the Lord and to fulfill His calling on your life no matter what.

A Person With Vision Has a Sense of Purpose

Proverbs 29:18 in the *New International Version* says, "Where there is no revelation, the people cast off restraint [perish]. . . ." The *Berkley* version says, "Where there is no vision the people run wild...."

The *King James Version* says, *"Where there is no vision, the people PERISH..."* (Prov. 29:18). What does the word "perish" mean here? It means to *go astray or be carried off.* A man with no vision has no future. He is carried off or led astray because he has no vision to keep him focused.

Let me give you an example from the Bible, taken from Exodus chapter 32. The children of Israel were in bondage in Egypt; they were slaves. And they were trying to get out, because they weren't free to serve the true and living God. While in Egypt, they had to serve the Egyptian god and cruel taskmasters.

Well, God sent a man, Moses, to lead them out of Egypt. In the Old Covenant, Jesus had not yet died for their sins so they could not go boldly to the throne of grace like we can today. So the Israelites' vision was directly linked to Moses.

God got them out of Egypt. He parted the Red Sea for them. He got them out with the Egyptians' money. And out of two to three million people, nobody was sick! God brought them out victoriously.

When Moses went up to Mount Sinai for forty days to commune with God, the people thought he had died. And since their vision was directly linked to Moses, their vision died in their eyes. What did they do? They went back to what they used to do. A man with no vision will always return to his past.

There used to be a television show called "The Fugitive." We could describe a fugitive as a man with no future or hope. If the police are looking for a fugitive, where is the first place they look for him? Some place linked to his past. The police will find out what he used to do, where he used to hang out, and the people he used to know. Why? Because they know he has no future. Therefore, they go to his past.

Your vision comes from prayer and spending time in the Word. It comes from staying built up in the Word and staying before the face of God in right relationship with Him. There are those people who just go to church, go home, and live the way they want. They don't have a relationship with God because they don't spend any time in the Word. Choose to be a person with vision. Be a person of the Word.

Don't Lose Your Focus

Once you receive a vision from God, you can still miss it from that point. Remember, God had given Abraham the vision of being the father of many nations. God told Abraham that it was His will for Sarah to conceive, although in the natural it seemed impossible. And Abraham believed God at first.

But we see in Genesis chapter 16 that Abraham got his eyes off God and onto his body. What happened? He lost his focus. When he was focused on God and God told him, "You will be the father of many nations," he didn't think about the impossible circumstances, such as their age or the barrenness of Sarah's womb. But the minute he got his eyes on his body and his wife's body, he lost his focus.

Abraham and Sarah started thinking and worrying. They tried to figure out God's plan on their own. Sarah came up with a plan. She decided that Abraham would become the father of many nations through another woman, not her. So she told Abraham to sleep with her handmaid.

Abraham slept with her handmaid and they had a baby. Then Sarah got upset and threw the handmaid and her child out of the house. Why did all this happen? They lost their focus.

Your focus should drive your vision. When Peter walked on the water, he was fine as long as his eyes were on Jesus. But when he looked at the wind-driven waves, he lost his focus — he took his eyes off Jesus — and he began to sink.

I have always wondered why women in labor have to breathe a certain way. I asked my mom and she said, "The doctors understand that if they can get a woman to focus on her breathing, she won't concentrate on the pain."

If you will keep your focus on God and the things of God, you won't have time to worry about what's going on around you. You won't concentrate on what So-and-so thinks or says, because you'll be focused on God and concentrating on Him.

As the Apostle Paul said, *"Being confident of this very thing, that he which hath begun a good work in you will perform it until the day of Jesus Christ"* (Phil. 1:6). God has placed you on this earth for a specific purpose. And He will complete that purpose He has begun in you if you will seek Him and stay focused on what He has called you to do. He will cause you to enter the ranks of the on-fire, redeemed people of God — a generation who will glorify His Name!

SECTION II

Chapter 4
A Special Note to PKs

Rev. Keith Butler II

Every one of us faces challenges in life to one degree or another that can affect whether we take our place in God or just give up and quit, going with the flow of the world. That's what many are doing today. In the face of challenges, they're succumbing to Satan, sin, and the world and are allowing circumstances to dominate them instead of dominating their circumstances.

But it doesn't have to be that way (that's one of the reasons we've written this book). Through an understanding of God and His Word, any person — young, "seasoned," or in-between — can rise above the challenges of life and fulfill his God-given destiny.

However, we believe it's necessary to address some of the particular challenges faced by those who are growing up or have grown up in a minister's home. Many PKs grapple in life with what is expected of them — from parents, from other Christians, and even from God. And Satan is not there to help! No, he knows that these children have the potential for greatness, for being mighty seeds sown in the earth. And he wants to hurt, hinder, and even destroy them. Preachers' kids need to know Satan's tactics and schemes to avoid the pitfalls and traps he will bring their way.

First, let's look at an important verse that outlines four responsibilities we all, especially PKs, need to fulfill: *"And that servant, which knew his lord's will, and prepared not himself, neither did according to his will, shall be beaten with many stripes"* (Luke 12:47).

In this verse are four responsibilities that are the foundation for being a successful PK: 1) *Commit yourself to being God's servant*; 2) *commit yourself to finding and knowing His will*; 3) *prepare yourself*; 4) *do His will*.

Then look at the next verse.

> **LUKE 12:48**
> **48 But he that knew not, and did commit things worthy of stripes, shall be beaten with few stripes. FOR UNTO WHOMSOEVER MUCH IS GIVEN, OF HIM SHALL BE MUCH REQUIRED: and to whom men have committed much, of him they will ask the more.**

We just read that the servant who knew his lord's will and prepared not himself, neither did according to his will, shall be beaten with many stripes. But he who knew *not* and committed things worthy of stripes, shall be beaten with *few* stripes. *"...For unto whomsoever much is given, of him shall be much required: and to whom men have committed much, of him they will ask the more."* This isn't a principle that just applies to this instance; this is a Kingdom principle. That means that it also applies to me and you.

A PK Is Especially Required To Be a Steward of What He's Received

First of all, I want you to notice that God gives great responsibility to those who have received much from Him. In general, this is a category PKs fall in. In other words, as a rule, they have more knowledge imparted to them than do other kids

2 TIMOTHY 2:1,2
1 Thou therefore, my son, be strong in the grace that is in Christ Jesus.
2 And the things that thou hast heard of me among many witnesses, the same commit thou to faithful men, who shall be able to teach others also.

Notice that in these verses, Paul is talking to his spiritual son Timothy. From reading this passage and Luke 12:48, we can learn two things: (1) People who have been given much have a great responsibility before God; and (2) God wants those who have received much to give much to others.

God expects more of the one who has grown up in the Word of God than He expects of the one who hasn't. Children who grow up in a minister's home usually know more about the things of God; they know that He is real, because they've been in His Presence and have experienced His power.

As a preacher's kid, I've known throughout my life, especially since entering the full-time ministry myself, that I could not do what everybody else was doing and please God. God gave me a certain responsibility at an age that could be considered early. It is a privilege as well as a responsibility, but it's not without its frustrations at times. Even in adulthood, there have been times I've said to Him, "Please, just let me be a normal, average young man." And God has always said, "No way."

I was never allowed by God to be "normal" or average for my age; I've always been treated as being older than I really was. Why? Because, spiritually speaking, I *was* older. I had an opportunity to mature in some of the things of God much earlier than you'd expect. As a result, I had to go ahead and make good use of that Word in my life, and I have never regretted it.

Let's look at an Old Testament verse that talks about stewardship in regard to spiritual things.

1 KINGS 19:19
19 So he departed thence, and found Elisha the son of Shaphat, who was plowing with twelve yoke of oxen before him, and he with the twelfth: and Elijah passed by him, AND CAST HIS MANTLE UPON HIM.

The mantle here is referring to the anointing. The anointing that was on Elijah's life was passed to Elisha, his spiritual son. But that anointing wasn't for Elisha's amusement. No, he had to serve God with that anointing. God expected much of Elisha. God required that Elisha carry on the work of his predecessor, Elijah.

Similarly, preachers' kids usually have their parents' anointing. The mantle or anointing gets placed upon them, too, and if the children are faithful, they will eventually have even more anointing than their parents had. They may receive a double portion as Elisha did (2 Kings 2:9-12). But at the same time, God will require a "double portion" of obedience too!

Anyone who's genuinely yoked up with his spiritual father, whether it's a natural father or a father in the Lord, has the mantle of his spiritual father upon him. So if God has given you a great anointing, He expects that anointing to be used in His service and for His glory, because He doesn't waste power.

As I said in a previous chapter, God has a dream, a plan, which can be summed up in this verse: *"And this gospel of the kingdom shall be preached in all the world for a witness unto all nations; and then shall the end come"* (Matt. 24:14). Jesus spoke these words during His earthly ministry, and God expects the Body of Christ to continue to work toward bringing this about.

God has a plan for the entire Body to spread the Gospel, but that means that He has a plan for *individual members* of the

Body to spread the Gospel. If a sports team is to be successful, individual team members must be successful too. Well, God has a design for our lives individually. He wants us to find and fulfill that plan and design so that He can place us like pieces of a puzzle in every "nook and cranny" — every village, town, city, state, district, province, and country — in *every* place all over the world!

God has already started the process. He has put a part of the vision in one person's heart, and another part of the vision in another's. Each one has in him the vision to be the best he can be in his field and to influence others for good to the glory of God. One man or woman might want to be the best movie director there is. Another might want to produce the first Christian movie that makes $100 million. Someone else might have the vision placed in his heart by God to be a Holy Ghost-filled President of the United States. God has a plan for reaching the world through those in the medical field, in legal and business professions, in industry, technology, agriculture, education, the sciences, the media, government, families, and churches and ministries.

The PK's Place in a God-Glorifying Generation

One intricate part of God's plan has to do with a combination of the latter three areas — families, churches, and ministries. I'm talking about men and women and their families who are involved as full-time clergy in churches and ministries. God will never waste the Word that's been sown into a person's life. He expects him or her to go out and do something good with that Word. And he gives that person the grace and strength to do it. We need to find out how to take hold of that grace and then take our place as men and women of God to help win that harvest of souls that God is waiting for.

So we know that when God gives you something, He requires responsibility. Yes, God does expect a little more from preachers' kids. You might not like that, but the sooner you settle that fact in your heart, the sooner you will begin to feel less frustrated and resentful. God's way is a good way — it's the *best* way! And He has a good life planned for you. Just realize that as a preacher's kid, you don't, as a rule, start out at the same starting line other people do. You should get a little head start. Therefore, God expects you to mature in certain areas quicker so you can accomplish more for His Kingdom.

The trouble occurs when the enemy challenges you and brings things across your path to try to stop you. That's why you have be vigilant (1 Peter 5:8). You can't sleep on the job, so to speak. You've been entrusted with much, and you have a great responsibility to guard and protect what you've been given. In the following chapters, we are going to specifically identify some challenges PKs face and talk about how to handle these challenges with the Word.

Chapter 5
A Day in the Life of a Preacher's Kid (For Parents of PKs) Part 1

Rev. Keith Butler II and Min. MiChelle Butler

Michelle Butler: To be a generation that's taking the work of God to the next level and glorifying His Name, you have to be a generation of people with fortitude and backbone — people who have faced challenges and have overcome. In this chapter, we're going to discuss several challenges that are unique to PKs, and in our discussion, we're going to address parents of PKs as well. The PK and his or her parents need to work together to ensure the success of a minister's family by ensuring the well-being of each member of that family.

Challenge Number One: The 'Fishbowl Syndrome'

The "fishbowl syndrome" is a big challenge in the life of a PK. You might ask, "What is the 'fishbowl syndrome'?" It is simply this: PKs, in a sense, live in a fishbowl. If you've ever seen a fishbowl, you know you can see right through it. Even if a fish moves from one side of the bowl to the other, you can still see the fish. It has nowhere to hide.

Similarly, the privacy and anonymity of a minister's child will for the most part be taken from him or her whether the child likes it or not. That child, even if he's very young, will be scrutinized and even judged by people because his parents are preachers.

When I was four years old, I didn't care about fashion. Now my younger sister, Kristina, is the fashion queen of our house, and I'm sure when she was four, she was picking out her clothes carefully! But I didn't care what I wore. And adults would watch me and judge my parents based on my appearance. But if you think about it, having to maintain a "perfect" preacher's kid presentation is a great expectation to place on a four-year old!

I experienced that same kind of frustration in the grade school I attended, which was a school my dad founded. I was smart and usually had the highest grade-point average in my class. Having a bit of a competitive edge, I worked hard to excel and to be the best I could be; I always wanted the best grade. One time I turned in an assignment I'd worked especially hard on, and received a B plus! I got really upset and went to the teacher. I said, "Why did I get a B plus? I've read some of the papers of kids who got an A, and I know mine was better. Why did I get this grade?" I knew my paper was an A paper, not a B-plus paper.

I never will forget what my teacher told me. She said, "Well, you did 'A' work, but because you're Keith Butler's kid, I graded you a little harder than the other students." Situations similar to this happened quite often.

It can be frustrating, discouraging, and disheartening to a young child for his efforts to go unrewarded. I could have become resentful and just given up and quit trying, but I had good parents who loved me, encouraged me, and gave me the Word. It caused me to rise up with a strong spirit, more determined than ever to win.

(Parent, most of the time, your young child won't look first to the Lord for protection and shelter in situations like this. Most young children do not have the ability to judge everything by the

Word and "edit out" things said to them that don't line up. They tend to believe everything adults tell them. Children look to their *parents* to be there for them and to love and encourage them. And that's your job — to always be there for your children.)

As a young child, there were also times in children's church when I would get pulled aside and disciplined because some of my friends were talking and being disruptive! The workers would say to me, "Your dad's a leader, so you should be a leader too. You should have told your friends not to talk during church."

Because I was Keith Butler's kid — a preacher's kid — I was never allowed to sit in the back of the classroom. The workers in children's church wanted to make me an example, and that's okay, but sometimes I felt as if I wasn't even permitted to be a kid!

I also remember going to friends' houses to spend the night, and often I would hear their parents saying to their own daughters, "Why can't you be more like her?" That put so much pressure on every child involved. Those parents didn't even know me — all they knew was that I was a preacher's kid.

Ultimately, I had a lot of problems with friends who grew up to despise me because I was always used to be their standard. They became resentful because they felt they never measured up, and I became resentful because of the unnecessary expectations and pressures put on me to be everything people thought I should be. It made me very uncomfortable at times, and it's feelings like this that can turn a child inward. Parents need to be observant enough to protect and pray for their children so that those pressures don't affect them in a negative way.

Now we all know that the ministry is a people business. If you're in the ministry and do not love people, you are in the wrong business. But there can be temptations for children of ministers to feel anything but loving toward people. It's important for parents of PKs to spend time with their children and to know what's going on with them. Many wrong decisions made and wrong paths taken by PKs could have been avoided if parents had stepped in early on to provide love, understanding, guidance, and a listening ear.

I love my parents, and I have happy childhood memories. They cared for us children above everyone else and made us feel loved and secure. They not only provided for our emotional security, but for our physical security and safety too. For example, my parents would not let me spend the night at anyone's house if they didn't know the parents. I mean, they checked those people out!

But when I would invite friends over, it seemed most of the parents never checked us out. The only thing some of them were interested in checking out was the Butlers' house and how my bedroom was decorated. That can put a lot of pressure on a kid, especially when you find out as a young child that not everyone likes you for who you are.

Preachers and preachers' kids need to be led concerning who they hang out with. Not everyone has pure motives. For example, some parents will push their kid off on a preacher's kid, using the situation to get to the PK's parents. If you are a minister who has children, you need to realize that some people will use their kids to get to you. Some people are enamored with your child's name and his or her association with you. This is very difficult for children to understand when they're younger, but they can experience a rude awakening when they're older, because they usually end up getting hurt at some point.

It's pressures like these that cause many PKs to rebel. But it can be avoided by nurturing a close family relationship between parents and children.

Another thing that causes PKs to rebel against God is wrong priorities on the part of the parents. Remember I said that the ministry is a people business. And, yes, when people are hurting, it's not always during office hours! PKs are called upon to make a lot of necessary sacrifices for the sake of the ministry, but if a minister is consistently counseling someone for five or six hours after a church service has ended, his family can grow to resent that. And it's even worse when the people needing counseling and taking up all of that minister's time are the ones who are making the PK's life miserable! Those people don't even like the minister's children; they judge them, criticize them, and put all kinds of unnecessary pressure on them. Yet those same people have no problem monopolizing the parents' time and telling them how much they love *them*.

Don't Let Your Children
Become a Generation Resenting God

It can be very easy for a PK to develop resentment toward people. It takes understanding and the loving guidance of the PK's parents to help him overcome certain attitudes he may have developed. Without that love and guidance, their child could end up losing out with God. God could say to that PK, "I want you to go into the ministry," but the PK might end up saying, "I'm not interested." In some cases, he would rather disobey God than answer a call to minister to people he has grown to disrespect.

Sometimes, living in a fishbowl can seem unbearable for a PK, especially a teenaged PK. The expectations can be not only unreasonable, they can be *impossible*! For example, a PK could avoid a lot of problems if he had no friends and was never seen in public with anyone — *ever*!

Let me explain what I mean. One time when I was a teenager, someone went to my mother and told her that I was behaving inappropriately with two guys! The woman who did this did not bother to validate her story. Actually, there was nothing to validate, because all she saw was me walking down a back hallway in one of the older ministry buildings with my two male cousins! At the time, there were some problems with teenagers being caught loitering in the bathrooms during services. There were a lot of out-of-the-way passageways in the old church, and the kids would use them to hide. But this woman saw us walking and, really, she made up the rest! We weren't hiding, and we weren't behaving inappropriately. We were just walking!

Even at that age in my life, I had a tremendous respect for the house of God, the church, and I didn't attend church to loiter or make trouble. That was never my motive. And, thankfully, my mom came to find that this woman's story wasn't true. But it was very traumatic for me, anyway. Never in my wildest dreams would I have ever thought someone would do something like that. But it happened. I'm not saying that children of lay people are never falsely accused, but this is the kind of thing a preacher's kid has to endure more often than other kids do.

Keith Butler II: As parents of PKs, you need to validate the stories people tell you about your children. People will come to you and tell on your kids — whether the kids did anything wrong or not! I mean, they'll tell you that your kids are doing everything from flying to the moon to shooting people! And, believe it or not, sometimes they fabricate things just to get a chance to talk to you. Also, it seems some people especially love to see ministers coming down on their children. It's almost as if these people are trying to divide the minister's family. But a family that's close will not fall prey to these injustices.

Even if your child does do something wrong and gets into trouble, keep the discipline private. Don't discipline your children in front of others. It's sad, but your child getting a spanking in church is very entertaining to some adults.

In general, everything that a preacher's kid does is seen or observed. Even if you as a PK are four years old, somebody is watching you. If you are *six* years old, somebody's watching you. If you're *eight* years old, somebody's still watching you! If you're *ten* or *twelve*, somebody's watching you, and if you're a teenager, people are *really* watching you! And they don't stop watching you even after you're grown.

Now people watch with different or varying motives. Some people are watching because they need a godly example. There's nothing wrong with that unless they tell a ten-year old that he is their example for living right! A ten-year-old PK has probably been raised in the Word, but chances are, he's not consciously trying to be anybody's example or role model (nor does he want to be). He's just minding his own business, living what he's been taught — and he's just being a ten-year old! (Often, being ten entails nothing more than having fun and trying not to get a spanking!)

Although it's true that as a PK grows older, stewardship is required by *God* of him, it's *not* true that *other people* should get to impose their own requirements and place impossible expectations on PKs. It is important to remember that a preacher's kid is a kid first! It is so unfair to place undue expectations on children of preachers, expecting them to be more smart, more holy, and more mature. Sometimes I think people view young PKs as they do the parents, expecting these children to be "mini preachers"! But you're asking for big-time trouble when you expect a child to act like an adult.

I'm not insinuating that all lay people place unrealistic expectations on preachers' kids. And our purpose for saying all this is not to try to persuade people to stop picking on PKs! Our primary purpose for writing this is to inform *parents* of PKs so that they can be better prepared to step in when they see certain warning signs indicating that their children need their help and support.

For example, if you're a minister with children, and you notice that suddenly your children don't want to go to church, just forcing them to go without sitting down and finding out what's going on with them would be unfortunate. The reason they don't want to go is probably because somebody is giving them trouble somewhere. You need to show them how much you care by getting to the root of the problem and then by taking care of it. A child is not equipped to deal with pressure the way an adult is, and without your help, a child certainly cannot respond to pressure being put on him by an adult.

So pay extra attention to your children if they begin to withdraw from church activities. Church is supposed to be as fun and meaningful for them as it is for the other children who attend. Don't permit them to be cheated out of what God has for them by leaving them to face pressure alone.

MiChelle Butler: I remember one time when I was twelve, my dad heard me crying in my room. I was prospering in school; in fact, I was at the head of my class. Everything seemed fine on the outside, but I was hurting on the inside.

I told my dad that I never wanted to go to school again. He sat down with me and just began to talk and ask questions. I didn't know how to articulate my feelings. The pressures of unrealistic and unfair expectations were a way of life to me, so I didn't know things could be different. I thought the things I was experiencing were just the way life was.

My dad stayed with me until I could communicate what I was feeling. I remember the words just came gushing out as I poured out my heart to him. My dad is a strong man, but he had tears in his eyes as he listened. He took immediate action. He took me out of the school I was in and got me away from the people who were putting pressure on me. He later told me that if he'd only known earlier what I was going through, he would have done something about it for me then.

I couldn't love God and people the way I do today without my parents' love and the time they took with me even when so many demands were being placed on them in the ministry. I am proud and pleased to serve God in the ministry today, but I can also see how things could have been much different if my mom and dad hadn't intervened in my life from time to time and helped me through some very trying situations.

Three Warning Signs To Notice

My brother alluded earlier to the fact that parents of PKs need to be alert and aware, responding quickly to warning signs in their children's lives. One sign he mentioned was withdrawal from or avoidance of church and its activities. A *second* warning sign is one I touched on, and that is resentment of the people in the church or of people in general.

A *third* warning sign is being overly introverted in a church or public setting. In other words, it's good and right to train a child not to be rambunctious in church, but if your child undergoes a complete personality change between home and church, you need to check it out. If he is acting *too* perfect in front of others and only acts like himself in private or when he's at home, problems could develop from that over time.

Yes, PKs do have a big responsibility to live what they've been taught. And since most of them grow up around the Word, they are accountable for what they do with that Word that's been put into their lives. They have the opportunity to be a great influence on others, and more is expected of them. But this responsibility can be over-emphasized and become a super source of pressure.

Sometimes even parents of PKs are guilty of pressuring their children beyond what is normal. For example, instead of stressing good manners *wherever* they are, they will tell their children, "You'd better not embarrass me in public. My reputation is on the line." Their motive is to keep themselves from being embarrassed, but over time, those children may develop resentment toward their parents and the public.

Besides that, if all the parents are thinking about is pleasing people and having a certain "front" in public, the children will think their parents are acting fake. When they're in public, the children will have the attitude, *Okay, I'm around people now, so let me change who I am so I don't embarrass my parents.* Parents who pressure their kids that way are missing it in training their children. They are teaching them to behave with the motive of not embarrassing them instead of with the motive of honoring God. If their parents teach them that they love them and God loves them, and if they teach their children to honor God, obedience to their parents will follow.

Motive is the key word here. A parent's responsibility is to train his child in the way that he should go, not to train the child not to embarrass him! A parent shouldn't say to his child, "I'm a preacher, and if you don't live right, people won't listen to me. So live right." What that is saying is, "You do what's right so my ministry can flourish," not, "Do what's right so you can be blessed of God and learn to walk in His blessings." There is a big difference, and it's a crucial difference.

Also, if you as a parent of PKs have other people who act as caregivers to your children, even overnight while you're away, make sure they are not pressuring your kids. You need to be careful who you have watch your children. The people who are closest to your children need to be people the children feel safe with, not pressured by.

We'll talk more about that later, but the bottom line is, allow your children to be children and don't let others put expectations on them that are unreasonable. Encourage your children to be themselves and to *like* themselves. Their self-image or how they see themselves will make or break them later in life whether they're called to the ministry or not.

Now I'm not making excuses for PKs who grow up and rebel against God and their parents. An adult PK is responsible for his actions, and he alone, not his parents, is accountable to God for what he does with his life. So if you're a PK with "issues," I encourage you to deal with or find help dealing with them now. Don't take your PK issues into adulthood. The sooner you let go of bad attitudes and realize that God is really the only One you have to please, the sooner you will move forward spiritually and enjoy the good life He's called you to.

As an adult, you are to seek to please God even before your parents. And the main way to please God is to walk by faith in close fellowship with Him and to develop in love. The greatest thing in the Kingdom of God is love, so we all need to strive constantly to develop and maintain our love walk.

That doesn't mean loving only the people who are nice to you and who love you. No, it means loving and serving the same people who talk behind your back and who are just waiting for you to mess up so they can say, "Aha!" These people want to have the attitude, *That preacher can't tell me anything about child-raising. His kids are hellions!* They aren't interested in being taught or helped themselves. They only want to see other people fail, because it makes them feel better about themselves.

As a PK, you have to be so close to God that you can love others unconditionally even as He loves unconditionally, especially if you are a minister. That love will motivate you to get up in the middle of the night before a meeting and pray for the people you're going to minister to. Love will cause you to sacrifice sleep to pray that you'll carry the anointing that God has for the people so that their needs will be met. Love will cause you to "lay down your life" for others, even those who have hurt you. So develop in love, because a ministry without love is not a ministry.

Challenge Number Two:
The 'Doorway Syndrome'

The "doorway syndrome" is what PKs experience when others view them as an opportunity — an open door — to advance. I talked about this briefly regarding people using their kids to befriend PKs for the sole purpose of getting close to the PK's parents.

PKs are not immune from this syndrome at any stage of their life, and it can come at them from all different directions for different reasons. For example, as a teenager, I had girls who wanted to be my friend in order to get to my brother! He wasn't even a minister at the time, but people could see it coming. I mean, he's the heir; his name is Keith Butler II. He bears my father's name, and everyone thinks that, eventually, he will take over the operation of the Word of Faith ministries.

A lot of mothers and daughters had their eye on my brother. I mean, what a powerful position a woman would be in to be the wife of Keith Butler II. It sounds silly, but it was as if girls were vying to be named the wife of the heir to the throne! My brother and I are close, and girls would try to befriend me to literally get their foot in the door — in the door of my house so they could be around my brother!

It's sad that some parents will use their own children if it means a chance for them to get close to certain people. That's why I said that PKs need to be led concerning who they hang out with. And if a PK is a young child, his or her parents should be discerning when it comes to their child's friends. Young children just want to have friends. They need the wisdom and discretion of their parents in selecting good, God-given friends.

Speaking from experience, I remember that as a child, I just wanted to have friends in school. And I did have many friends, but they didn't all stick around. Some abandoned me when their curiosity about my family was satisfied enough. Now as a child, I didn't view that as people using me; I looked at it as, as soon as people get to know me, they leave me. I simply saw it as rejection.

We know that people can try to use a PK to get close to the PK's parents or other family members. But they can also try to use a preacher's kid to tell on someone else or to try to get something done that they want done. For example, some people are afraid to go directly to my father to complain about something or someone, so, often, they'll come to me instead and start painting a big picture of how bad the situation is. I've said to some of them, "Why don't you just go tell my dad?" They've said, "Oh, I don't want to bother him. It's not *that* important. Maybe you could just mention it to him."

Keith Butler II: It is a fact that people in a church will try to use the pastor's kids as a "doorway" to get what they want, whether it's a social relationship with the parents, the promotion of their ideas, or some type of advancement in the church hierarchy. The sad part of this is, if they don't get what they want, the kids are the ones who get hurt the most. Sometimes the people who get close to the PKs just "disappear," leaving the PKs to feel hurt and abandoned. At other times, the people begin treating the PKs poorly because they didn't get their way. One minute, they're "cool" with the kids; the next minute, they treat the kids like the enemy.

Can you see now why children of ministers need the close oversight and loving protection of their parents? There are some crazy people out there. And the people we're talking about are not out in the world — they are in the church!

Young children are too young to run to their Bible when something bad happens, open it, and say, "Okay, what does the Word say about this situation?" No, learning to look to the Word for themselves takes time. In the meantime, their parents are their protection.

MiChelle Butler: We've been presenting some hard facts and some practical, real-life information, not to get sympathy, but to help ministers and their families prepare for and deal with the challenges they will all face at one time or another. But PKs and their parents need balance in facing the challenges that are unique to the minister's family. For example, a PK who's been hurt by someone who befriended him with wrong motives may start to have the attitude, *Everyone is trying to use me.* When others are friendly toward him, he may think, *Why did they talk to me? What do they want?*

That's why it's so important to be led by the Spirit of God. I like a particular verse from Colossians chapter 3: *"And let the peace of God rule in your hearts, to the which also ye are called in one body; and be ye thankful"* (v. 15). You need to be led by peace. God's peace is the answer.

Some people, even ministers, think they don't need to pray or be led in this area, because they think they can judge the character of a person well enough not to be deceived by him. But they are wrong. People and situations can come along that are attractive and appealing, and even the sharpest people can be misled. I mean, a PK wouldn't fall into the wrong crowd or get involved with the wrong person if something about those people wasn't attractive to the PK.

The answer isn't always obvious. That's why we need the Holy Spirit, God's peace, to lead and guide us and keep us in balance. We need to learn to trust Him and not lean to our own understanding. When He says something, we don't need to reason it out or wait until we get an explanation before we obey. It's better to obey immediately and avoid trouble than to have to deal with the complications of a wrong decision later.

Challenge Number Three:
The 'Low Self-Esteem Syndrome'

The next challenge PKs invariably face is what I call the "low self-esteem syndrome." I'm not saying that all preachers' kids have poor self-images, but I am saying that there will be assaults on their self-esteem that they will either rise above or succumb to.

Satan will vigorously attack the self-esteem of a PK. It's not that Satan hates only ministers' kids; he will attack the self-esteem of anyone, young and old alike. But because of the Word that's in their heart, he will persecute PKs and prey on their weaknesses, magnifying those weaknesses beyond what is normal.

One of the biggest devices he uses against PKs is thoughts of their own worthlessness apart from their parents. Parents of PKs — ministers — are so often given sort of a celebrity status by people, and this can cause the children to feel overshadowed. In other words, the more well-known a minister becomes, the more "lost in the shadows" the children can feel. That is why you often see adult PKs out trying to "find themselves" instead of serving God. At some point in time, they lost their own sense of uniqueness — their identity or what defines them as a person — and now they're trying to get it back.

Certainly, Satan comes against a person by bringing thoughts to the person's mind. But he'll also use the lips of other people to verbalize those thoughts. Then his attack is on in full force. For example, people will actually say to a PK, "You're only where you are today because of your parents." There are times when a comment like that won't bother a PK, because, in reality, *all* parents, whether they are ministers or not, should nurture and influence their children for good, helping them to find their niche in life and helping them succeed in any way they can. I don't know of any parent who doesn't want his children to have a better life than he had, even if he had it good growing up.

But there are times when that kind of comment hurts a PK, especially if he's in his teen years or he's already struggling with developing his own identity and making his own mark in the world.

I remember I had a hard time with this in my teen years. There was a time when it seemed I was never referred to as MiChelle Butler, only Keith Butler's daughter. I became so frustrated that when someone asked me who I was, I just said, "I'm Keith Butler's daughter." I did that because I thought that MiChelle Butler was a nobody. But deep down, I knew that wasn't true, and that's why I was angry. I even began to resent my dad because of it and eventually got to the point where I didn't want to go anywhere with him. I didn't want him attending my school events and activities, either, because everyone knew him, and I was tired of being identified only as Keith Butler's daughter.

Even when I left the school my dad had founded as a part of his ministry, that feeling of low self-esteem followed me. I began looking for places to be where no one would know me as Keith Butler's kid.

This is where preachers' kids can fall away from God. They're looking for places where they can "escape," and some of those places are good in general (such as a school club where the other members don't know anything about the PK). But a PK may also begin looking in places that are *not* good. You see, out in the world at the nightclubs, the people who hang out there don't care who your father is. This holds a great deal of attraction for the PK who is wrongly believing that his entire self-worth is based on his parents and their accomplishments.

If PKs allow their identity to be tied solely to their parents and the fact that their parents are ministers, those PKs are going to fall into Satan's trap. They're going to go off in search of a name for themselves, and they're going to get as far away from the church as they can to do it!

This is one of Satan's biggest tricks, because you *don't* have to go away from the things of God to "find" yourself. You see, Satan has a lot of PKs running, and they're going in the wrong direction. His goal is to steal from them their true identity — who they are in Christ because of their union with Him.

I mean, Satan is not going to have PKs running to the Church and to Christians! He's going to remind them that Church is the place where they felt out of place and useless in the first place. So they begin running with people who aren't interested in God and don't want to hear anything about Him. These people aren't impressed with the PKs' parents and don't want to hear about *them*, either. And *that's* what PKs on the run find so appealing. They feel they can be accepted for themselves, apart from their parents' identity, and that they can establish their own identity completely separate from their parents.

Even PKs who aren't running want their own identity, and that's not wrong; everyone needs to have his or her own identity. But there are some wrong ways to go about having your own identity and making your mark. That's why prayer is so important. You need God's wisdom to know, first, that this is a self-esteem issue and, second, how to deal with it properly.

To have your own identity, you have to be yourself. This is where some PKs miss it. They try so hard to be *completely* different from their parents that they can't be themselves. They may be like their parents in some respects, but they will deny or squelch those aspects of their personality, and this can be very harmful to their self-esteem.

Some PKs don't want to answer God's call to the ministry for the simple reason that their parents are in the ministry, and they don't want to appear to be copy-catting their parents or riding their coattails, so to speak.

One of the first messages I preached as a new minister became a milestone in my life that I will never forget. I realized that day that I was a lot like my father — more like him than I'd ever realized before. And I recognized that I minister a lot like he does. I'm sure part of it is due to our close association in ministry and his anointing that has come upon my life. Another part of it is, he is my father, and we are a lot alike!

In my message, I remember I made an opening statement that my father makes all the time. Well, the congregation just burst out laughing. They laughed because I sounded just like my dad. Now they weren't being cruel; they just recognized the familiarity of the statement, and I think it helped break the ice, so to speak, and establish a rapport with them.

As I continued to minister that message, I felt the Spirit of God moving, and I knew I was ministering to the hearts of the people. The fact that most of my message had been preached by my dad (and other ministers) at some point in the past made it no less anointed.

That was a big night for me. Many were blessed, and they commented to me what a great message it was. But my success turned bittersweet when I received my first piece of ministry mail shortly afterward. The person writing asked, "Can't you think for yourself? Are you truly called by God, or are you just being trained to take over a 'dynasty'?"

Now in the past, that would have devastated me. You see, I was one of those PKs who tried for a long time to deny my call to the ministry because of what people might think and because I wanted my own identity — something to do in life that was far removed from ministry. I didn't run from the church, but I did run from the call to the ministry.

I was actually already in college when I finally answered that call. I was doing well in school, but I began seeking the Lord in prayer daily because, deep down, I wanted to do His will. Every day, I prayed a half an hour in my dorm room. Now thirty minutes at a time was "deep" for me back then — that was a lot of praying for me!

It took about a month and a half to find out where God wanted me to be. But when I found out, I knew that I knew it was God, and I was determined to obey. He told me to go to RHEMA Bible Training Center, and I was RHEMA-bound! People tried to talk me out of it. They couldn't understand why I would just up and leave college when I was doing so well. Some even said, "Your dad is making you go, right? He finally got to you, didn't he?"

When you're struggling as a teenager to find your place and your own personal identity, Satan will try to use that against you.

For example, if you're seeking God and making some decisions about what you believe God wants you to do, Satan will use people to come against you or to try to influence you in the wrong direction. *Everything good that you decide to do for God, Satan will try to undermine.*

In my case, I could have said, "Forget it. I don't want to be just 'Keith Butler's daughter.' I don't want to travel the same path he has traveled. I'm not going to RHEMA. I'm not going to do this." But, fortunately, because I'd sought God so intently, I knew for myself what I was supposed to do. No "flesh and blood" revealed it to me; no man told me what to do. *God* told me, and, as a result, I had the attitude, *I'm called of God, and no matter what happens or what anyone says, God is number one in my life, and it's what He says that's important.*

When I stand before the throne of God one day, I don't want to say to Him, "Lord, I didn't do what You told me to do because everybody was talking about me." To hear Him say, "Well done, thou good and faithful servant" is what motivates me in life. So at the time I read that unkind letter, I was confident enough in my calling and determined enough to obey it that I could just let those words go without thinking on and on about them.

Although it wasn't my first challenge as a preacher's kid, that was my first big hurdle in the ministry. But getting past that only solidified some things in my life and made me even stronger than before. I can accept the fact that not everyone will like me and that there will even be those who criticize me. And I am okay with the fact that I am like my father! As long as I'm being myself, it's okay that I minister and act like him at times. I'm proud of my dad, so why wouldn't I want to be like him?

Keith Butler II: A PK will have self-esteem issues. I didn't say those issues would get the best of him or her, but they will present themselves as a temptation and will have to be dealt with at some point.

It's amazing that a PK can grow up around the Word and still have no idea of his personal self-worth. How the PKs' parents minister to them can greatly affect whether they will grow up well-adjusted and happy or discontented and confused. Parents of PKs should constantly build up their children and make them feel good about themselves. PKs should feel successful in their own eyes and special to their parents and to God.

Parents of PKs need to teach their children how precious they are to God and that they've been bought with a great price. Children should understand that Jesus shed His blood for them as much as He did for their parents. Some children of ministers can grow to feel as if they were only "let in" under the umbrella of mama and daddy. The truth behind the phrase "accepted in the beloved" (Eph. 1:6) can be impersonal to them, and the fact that God loves them with an everlasting love can be foreign to their thinking. So the most important revelation PKs can have is that they are a unique, beloved son or daughter of God *before* they are a preacher's kid.

Chapter 6

A Day in the Life of a Preacher's Kid
(For Parents of PKs)
Part 2

Rev. Keith Butler II and Min. MiChelle Butler

MiChelle Butler: In this chapter, we're going to continue talking about the life of the PK and the unique challenges he or she faces daily. We concluded the previous chapter with a PK's third challenge — the low self-esteem syndrome, a challenge the PK, with the help of his or her parents, must be aware of and stand against continually in order to overcome.

Besides the identity crisis a preacher's kid will face is a similar self-esteem issue that is a bit more subtle. It has to do with being a people-pleaser. Because he comes in contact with so many people, a preacher's kid knows that people expect him to be spiritual and to act a certain way. That's why you see a lot of PKs who are two-faced. They'll come to church and know exactly who to talk to, what to say, and how to act. They'll put on a certain face at church and do whatever it is they need to do to get people to like them, because they don't like themselves.

Closely connected with this challenge of maintaining a healthy sense of self-worth is challenge number four, one of two more challenges we'll be discussing in this chapter. This challenge deals with the fear of letting people get to know you for fear of letting them down.

Challenge Number Four: The Fear of Failing The Expectations of Others

Because of the grand expectations placed upon children of ministers, a PK can easily fall into the trap of trying to be someone he's not in an effort to impress others. Once taken by this snare, he is certain no one — not even God — would like him if they knew his true personality, the one thing that gives him his identity as a valuable and unique creation of God. In attempting to escape from the lie he has created, the PK will often run from God and from the people who are most important to him.

A PK must learn to recognize his own identity and calling apart from that of his parents. With the proper guidance, children can do this successfully without too many bumps and scrapes along the way. A child who grows up confident of his parents' love, of God's love, and of His value in Christ will avoid this dangerous pitfall of getting into fear over the expectations of others.

When you see a certain celebrity on TV or in the movies, you usually attach some expectation to that person of what he or she is really like. Most of the time, those expectations are unrealistic. Celebrities are a good example of people who portray images that are not real.

For example, you might see a man in a movie who is the perfect gentleman. He always knows exactly what his woman wants. He knows exactly what to say and when to say it. He's always sensitive, romantic, and he never offends her. He's not only handsome, he's perfect! But, in reality, if you met that celebrity — the man who played that role in the movie — you would be let down. He might have some good qualities in real life, but you'd find that he's not what you thought he was. He wouldn't be that perfect person he portrayed in the movie.

Many times, the same thing goes for preachers' kids. People will paint a certain picture of what they think the PKs are like. These people will look at the minister and think, *He's a great preacher. His kids are probably great kids who never misbehave.*

As I said before, some of my friends' parents always thought I was perfect. They wanted their kids to be just like me before they even got to know me. Why? Because they had a certain image built up in their minds of what I was like.

This can be hard on the PK. If he is not taught properly and lovingly nurtured in the Word, he can develop poor self-esteem because he constantly feels like if he's not on his best behavior, he will destroy the image and let people down. And that would be devastating to the PK who just wants to please people and make them happy. He thinks, *If people get to know me, they'll get let down.* So he puts on a front in public, constantly striving to keep up the image. Before long, he's hurting on the inside and disliking himself more and more.

Let me show you how unreasonable expectations can hurt the person the expectation is attached to as well as the person who has the unreasonable expectation. Not too long ago, a girl I know had just gotten saved and was very hungry for the Word. She wanted to know everything she could about God. She wanted to know how to make her life better. She was constantly asking questions, and she wanted to go with me wherever I went.

One time I took her out with a group of my friends to eat lunch after a Sunday morning service. In the service that morning, a woman walked in wearing an outfit that I'll just say was attention-getting, but not in a good way! It was the kind of outfit you'd see and then quickly turn your head the other way because you didn't want to make a comment about it or burst out laughing, especially if you caught someone's eye who was also noticing this fashion fiasco!

Later at lunch, someone did finally say something about the woman's hat. The rest of us laughed at her comment, and we went on talking about something else. We were just relaxing together and having fun as a group of eighteen and nineteen year olds, but the girl who'd just gotten saved began to withdraw and act depressed. Later she told me that I discouraged her walk with God because her idea of what my life was like had been shattered. She said she never would have thought that I would laugh at someone's hat or say that it was ugly, because everything is beautiful in God's eyes. Now I'm not talking about drinking or taking drugs and causing someone to stumble — I'm talking about laughing at an ugly hat!

I'm not justifying talking or laughing about someone's appearance or their taste in fashion. I'm simply making the point that preachers' kids can have a difficult time if they're always "stiff," trying to impress others and never getting to let their hair down, so to speak, and just be real. That young Christian was defining her Christianity by me — or by her *expectations* of me. The expectations of others can be difficult, even impossible, to live up to.

That's why it's so important to know that before you are a PK, you are a son or daughter of God. You had a purpose before you were born to your parents. And, you know, it's not by chance that you were born into the family you were born into. And since it's God's idea and plan that you as a PK stand at the forefront of this generation in taking His Kingdom to another level, He must have known that you could do it! So get your PK issues squared away now. Don't take them with you into the future. If you're young, don't let those things tag along with you into adulthood. Don't try to take those problems with you to the next level; they will only hinder you if you do.

One way you will develop as a person and mature into adulthood is by holding yourself, not your parents, accountable and responsible for your life. You have to decide that no matter what your parents have or have not done, you're going to obey and serve God. You have to decide that even if they stopped obeying God, you're going to continue on. You're going to find and take your place in this God-glorifying generation that's going to do greater things for Him than have ever been seen before. Forget the people who have persecuted you and who are just waiting in anticipation for you to mess up. Stop blaming others and making excuses for why you aren't where you should be. Just get up and get there — God will help you do it!

I can confidently say that, while my parents were great examples as ministers and parents, my relationship with God is really why I am where I am today. There were times in my life when I was not excited about the Word. I went to church, but it just wasn't "clicking." My parents never beat me over the head with the Word. They gently guided me, letting me come into my own so that I could develop and enjoy a personal relationship with God for myself. Today if a backslider blames me for his Christian walk and tells me it's my fault he's going to hell, I can run to God for myself, and He can help me! He can minister to me and even show me how to restore that backslider to the faith.

If I didn't have that relationship with God, I might to run to my parents, and they would help me. But they couldn't sustain me day in and day out amidst the pressures of life. Without God's help, I would eventually fall away from serving Him, because no man can give you the kind of confidence you need to stay put in your calling when the pressure is on. You have to get your self-worth from God. And if you're a minister with children, that means you have to get your self-worth from God, too, because kids do what they see.

You see, ministers have pressures that come with being in the ministry. My parents are no exception. But if they had not handled those pressures by going to God and finding out who they were in Him, chances are I would not know how to do that, either. The things I heard them preach would have been just another good sermon. It would have been a lot harder to live it if I had not witnessed them living and putting into the practice the things they ministered.

The bottom line is, whether you're a preacher, a preacher's kid, or both, your value must be attached to God. Your worth must be found in Him if you're going to make it in life.

One of the greatest things parents can do for their children is to teach them how to develop a relationship with God and to hear from Him for themselves. And if you're a minister, you need to let your child discover the call of God on his or her own life. You may know there's a call on your child's life, but you have to let him discover it for himself.

If a PK pursues the ministry based on what his parents have told him to do, then when persecutions and the storms of life arise, he won't be able to resist the temptation to throw in the towel and quit. Uncertainty and confusion will only compound problems he's had with his self-esteem. He will feel like a failure and won't know where to turn for help. He needs the solid foundation of having heard God for himself to be able to stand strong. He needs to know that he can run to God and that God will always be there for him and never let him down.

It was a great day when I realized that God will speak to me like He speaks to my father. I heard from God for myself about my call to the ministry. I was nervous about telling my parents, because they had never said a word to me about the ministry. In fact, when I was younger and people would say to me, "Have you ever thought about going into the ministry?" I'd tell my parents, and do you know what they'd say to me? They'd answer, "Oh, isn't that something" or "Isn't that nice." For the longest time, I'd wanted to be a professional flautist, and they'd always supported my dreams and goals. They never tried to influence me toward the ministry.

When I did finally go to my parents to tell them God had spoken to me about the ministry, it took me about a half an hour to get it out. They sat there patiently while I cried and tried to tell them what I'd experienced. They knew what I was going to say, but they waited for me to say it.

There is so much wisdom in the way they handled that, because, now, no matter what happens, I know that I'm called. There is no doubt in my mind that I'm called to the ministry, and I know who called me. My mom did not call me. My dad did not call me. My *brother* did not call me. *God* called me, and I heard from Him for myself.

My parents never said anything to me or my brother about the ministry. In fact, at one time, Keith, or André, as I call him, wanted to be an aerospace engineer. My dad took the time and money to send him to NASA to get a first-hand look at what that kind of career would entail. As I said, my parents totally supported me when I wanted to be a flutist. I mean, my flute cost more that a lot of people's cars! But they bought it for me because I needed a professional model in order to compete. They sent me to music camps and enrolled me in college to pursue a music degree.

What were my parents doing? They were demonstrating confidence in us and in God. They knew we would be hungry to do God's will, and they knew God would speak to us about His plan and purpose for our lives.

The Bible says, *"Train up a child in the way he should go: and when he is old, he will not depart from it"* (Prov. 22:6). When they quote that verse, some people want to emphasize spanking a child when he's bad or has misbehaved. But if you believe this verse concerning the discipline part — that when the child is old, he will not depart from the way he's been trained to go — you have to believe that the Word that's been put in your child as a part of his "training" will come out when he needs it. You have to believe that that Word will guide and direct him in his actions, in the direction he takes, and in all the affairs of life.

A child will not depart from the Word that's been put in his heart as a part of his training in righteousness. The key is, you as a parent have to allow that Word to come out. You have to allow that Word to do what it's supposed to do in your child's life. You have to have confidence in that Word that it will produce in your child a foundation that cannot be shaken.

As a result of the Word that's been put in my life, I knew what to do to find God's direction for my life. I knew to pray and seek Him about what He'd have me to do. And because of that Word, I can't be shaken in my calling.

If my dad had tried to tell me years ago that I was called to the ministry, I might have resisted it, because I had other plans. And it may have taken me longer to discover God's will for my life. But, now, even if my dad said to me, "Baby, are you sure you're called to the ministry?" I'd just look at him like he was crazy — like he needed to do some extra praying!

I know beyond a shadow of a doubt what my calling is. For a PK — or *any* young person — to know for himself the direction God wants him to take in life is so important for his self-esteem and sense of value.

Keith Butler II: Growing up, I guess MiChelle and I wanted to be a little of everything! Before MiChelle dreamed of becoming a flutist, she wanted to be a pediatrician. My goals went from playing professional basketball to being an aerospace engineer to becoming a successful businessman after college. Every time we pursued a new dream, our parents didn't say, "No, you're called to preach." We never had a hint that we were called to preach until God told us.

I think that's the best way, because when people would come up to us and tell us they thought we were called to preach, we fought it. PKs don't need to hear from others, including their parents, what they are supposed to do in life. In fact, the minute a parent tells his child he's called to the ministry, that child will probably start running from it. He needs to hear from God, not from you, the parent about his calling. The calling on a person's life is a personal matter. It's between him and God, and the person needs to hear from God about it for himself.

In short, a PK must identify his own calling. As a parent of a PK, you may have great, lofty goals for your child, but you must allow him to discover his calling for himself. If you do, God will take care of the rest, and God's way is always the best way.

Challenge Number Five:
The Parent Challenge — Keeping
Your Priorities Straight and Your House in Order

MiChelle Butler: First Peter 3:1-7 talks about the husband and wife relationship. Verse 7 talks about a husband dwelling with his wife according to knowledge. In Genesis 1:28, the command God gave to Adam was to be fruitful and multiply, not to be *dysfunctional* and multiply!

God wants our families to be fruitful, happy, and productive. We need knowledge to function as He intended and to glorify Him in our families and in our lives individually. People are so zealous for more spiritual knowledge — sometimes so much so that they will swallow every new wind of doctrine that comes down the pike. But God wants us to have some practical knowledge from His Word concerning the home and family. Even though you're called to the ministry, before you're called to be a *minister's* family, you're called to be a *family*. So you need to seek God's knowledge in this area too.

You see, you have to be a fruitful family first before you can go out and effectively minister to others. You have to be a father first before you're a preacher. You have to be a mother first. *You are called to take care of your family first!* If you miss this important truth, all the good work you do in the ministry will be in vain. As one minister put it, "What good does it do to win the world if you lose your family in the process?"

A young child does not understand sacrificing for the sake of the ministry. Yet sacrifice is what so many children have been told that they're supposed to do. A young child does not understand the concept that he's giving up his daddy as a seed to the people in the church whom he must minister to. As I said before, children can grow to feel threatened by that prospect when the very people the man is ministering to are putting pressure on his kids. They can begin to feel as if Daddy is taking sides with those people against his own children!

All children are, in a sense, selfish by nature. They aren't born with certain characteristics in full bloom. They are still developing, and they need their parents. It is wrong for ministers to constantly allow people to take them from their children. The minister may see his sacrifices as noble. He may even be moved with compassion at people's needs. But he mustn't forget showing compassion to his offspring!

It is cruel and unwise when a parent consistently says to his child, "I can't come to your game" or "I won't be at your play" or "I can't tuck you in tonight." And it's especially unwise when he tells his child that the reason why is that people need Jesus. On top of feeling rejected and even abandoned by his parent, that child will resent Jesus and the church, because Jesus and the church are always taking his parents away from him along with priceless opportunities of doing things together as a family.

So even though you're called to the ministry, God has called you to be a family first.

My dad traveled when I was young, but I don't really remember it. In other words, it didn't negatively impact my life, because he didn't sacrifice us for his job responsibilities. In fact, he made huge sacrifices of his own time to make sure he was there when we woke up in the morning. Sometimes he had to wake us up before he left, but I always remember my dad being there.

Then when we were a little older, Dad had a certain opportunity that he considered taking. But it meant he'd have to travel more and be gone three days out of the week. He brought us all together and discussed it with us. We all agreed that he should take the opportunity and said we were willing to deal with his absence. But in the end, he didn't take that job.

These are the memories I have of my father. As important as the ministry is to him, he has cancelled meetings because one of us needed him. If he's in his office in a meeting and one of us calls, he answers the phone. I'm sure he feels torn at times. I mean, people are depending on him. He has a "mega" church with thousands of members whom he can't neglect. He deals with serious issues in people's lives every day. But he has never sacrificed us or made us feel second-class or "put on a shelf" while he set the world on fire! He is and always has been my dad before he's Bishop Keith Butler.

My dad has always been there for us, and I can't tell you what a blessing that's been to me and what it's meant to my life. Even in adulthood, I feel my father's care for me. One particular incident that happened recently might give you some idea of the type of man my father is and the sacrifices he made for us when we were children.

Once I became very sick when I was twenty years old and away at Bible college. I didn't call my dad because I knew that at the time, he was hosting a guest speaker from out-of-town who was ministering in the church. A pastor can't just up and leave his guest speaker! So I called to talk to my mom and told her what was going on. I said, "Don't tell Dad." She immediately put me on hold. When she came back to the phone, she said, "MiChelle, I just told your father. He's on his way."

At first, I was angry at my mom for telling Dad. There were many good people around me at Bible school who could have taken me to the doctor or hospital and helped me. But two hours later, there was a knock on my door, and it was my father. I mean, he left that minister in a minute! I felt bad about it. But I will never forget that incident as long as I live, because what my dad did was a statement of his love for me and was more meaningful than a thousand "I love you's." His actions demonstrated that I was his priority over his job (although the ministry is not just a job).

Now when my dad heard I was sick, he couldn't get a commercial flight out of town, so he had pay the extra money to charter a jet to get to me. He hadn't packed, so he was in his suit when he arrived. I was sick and was sleeping on the longer of two couches I had. My dad, who is six-feet, two inches tall, slept in his clothes on the shorter couch.

I was so sick, I couldn't walk very well. My dad stayed two and a half days, taking me to the doctor both days. Then he flew me back home for a while so he and my mom could take better care of me.

A lot of parents don't have a "whatever it takes" attitude about their children. But it's so important that parents demonstrate that kind of love to their children, because it will speak volumes to them, and they will never forget it. It will minister more to them than all the messages in the world.

I think it's especially important for fathers to give their daughters their time and attention. Because of all the time my father spent with me, I have never been "caught up" in a guy, getting myself trapped in an unhealthy relationship that could hurt and scar me emotionally. I'm not looking for love in all the wrong places, because I know that guys who aren't living one-hundred percent for God can't give me anything in the way of emotional security that I don't already have in my God and in my own natural father.

The important thing in developing and maintaining a strong family is to have a home life apart from the church. Have hobbies and interests that your family can pursue together. It may not sound spiritual, but your entire lives can't be about the church and the ministry. You'll burn out and fall apart as a family if you can't ever separate the two.

When my brother and sister and I were young children, my parents used to take us out to dinner once or twice a month (we didn't go out to eat as often as we do now). We would sit around the dinner table, and my dad would bring up a certain subject and say, "This is the topic we're going to discuss tonight." We didn't talk about the church or the ministry. The subject might be what kind of mate we would be looking for one day.

Now I was seven years old, but I remember those discussions! My dad would tell us important qualities to look for in a mate, such as having similar backgrounds, goals, and ideals, and we would talk about that for hours. The ideals and convictions we have today came about as a result of conversations we had with our parents when we were little children.

You see, you as a parent can't just force your ideals on your children. You have to discuss these things with them in a friendly setting and show them that you're genuinely interested in them. When your children feel loved and cared for, they will respect you and your beliefs, and they will want to listen to what you have to say.

Spending time together on a consistent basis also creates a bond in a family that lasts a lifetime and grows stronger as the years go by. The times we spent together as a family helped us kids make it through life. No matter what pressures we faced in the world around us, our home life was a shell of protection to us, a haven of rest and peace in which we felt safe and secure. In the face of problems, we had the attitude, *Just let me get home to my family.* There were five of us in the family, so if we ever felt like nobody else loved us, we knew we had four friends waiting at home who would never hurt or betray us.

Now that my brother is married, there are six of us, and we still have that bond. A strong family bond is so important in a day when you hear of sons betraying their own fathers — not just in business, but in the ministry too. It goes back to the home life, and it begins with the parents.

Children are parents' first responsibility over all their other responsibilities. Parents only have their children with them for a certain amount of time — for a season. Parents need to make the most of that time even if it means making sacrifices. Children have to know that they are their parents' number-one priority after their parents' personal relationship with God and with each other, and they need to know this from a very early age.

Even as an adult, I've seen my father making sacrifices for me and my brother and sister, because we are still his priority. For example, I played basketball at Bible college, and my dad would fly to my away games. He would leave staff meetings in Atlanta or Detroit and catch a plan to whatever city I was playing in. It's almost unheard of for a parent to go out of his way like that for his children.

I'm not saying that you as a parent have to spend exorbitant amounts of money or money beyond your means — or even go beyond certain other limitations you may have — to travel all over the country for your children. But there are things you can do to show them you're interested in their life and to make them feel special. For example, if your child is going out of town to participate in some event or activity you cannot attend, you could drive him to the bus or airport and wait with him until he leaves. You could wish him well and tell him you love him and that you'll see him when he returns.

A wise parent will see the short- and long-term value of making his child feel valued and loved.

Keith Butler II: The issue here is one of priorities. Some ministers' can become so "spiritual" that raising their children loses its priority status and becomes a side-thought. But, remember, you need to be a "normal" parent to your "normal" kids. Kids are normal; they are never too super-spiritual or too busy to kick back and have fun. They will *take* the time to have a good time! Some parents need to learn this lesson from their children!

In their teachings on the home and family, my parents teach that the priorities should be as follows: God first; family second; and ministry third. I agree. You might be saying, "Well, *of course*, that's true." But there are a whole lot of ministers who don't believe that! They take one scripture out of context in which Jesus says, "Who is My mother or My brothers?" (Matt. 12:48;

Mark 3:33) and try to use that to prove that ministry comes before family.

But it's that kind of thinking that causes kids to go astray and be all over the place — every place but where they should be. That the ministry comes before the family is simply not scriptural. First Timothy 3:4 and 5 outlines certain qualities of a bishop (or any minister) that must precede his office. Those qualities include running his house well and having his children in godly subjection. Verse 5 says, *"For if a man know not how to rule his own house, how shall he take care of the church of God?"*

In other words, you could say that these qualities are prerequisites for walking in that ministry office. A bishop must be a keeper or ruler over his own house, managing well his personal affairs, before he can be ruler or minister over a church.

As a minister, you have to have your priorities straight. You need to be the greatest parent you can be. You need to be involved in your children's lives. MiChelle shared about my dad attending her games when she played college basketball. I played college basketball, too, and he was at my games as well. But he didn't just start doing that when we were adults. He did that throughout our lives. He made a point of being at all our games when we were children. He acted just like a parent would who wasn't in the ministry. In other words, he didn't let the ministry take precedence over his family. He kept his priorities straight.

Some people think that training their children means constantly giving them Bible lessons and quoting the Word to them all day long. Some think that my dad wore a suit and tie all day long, even at home, and preached to us every day. But my father didn't push the Word down our throat, so to speak. Yet he gave us the Word day and night, as the Word commands (Deut. 6:7;11:19). He did it with his life. He gave us the Word by living the Word, by loving us and spending time with us, and by being real with us.

Kids don't want to hear five hundred scriptures. Yes, they need to hear the Word, but you have to put it to them in such a way that they can receive it, and you do that by being real with them. Talk about life issues in light of the Word and its principles (talk *with* them, not *to* them so that they don't become defensive). Teach children early what they need to look for in a mate. Show them while they're young how to handle money and work with a budget. Then when they're older, they'll remember these things. They'll know things as young adults that many don't learn until they're fifty!

If you're a PK or the parent of a PK, you know from firsthand experience that the ministry can be lonely. Other people can't relate to that, but it's true; the ministry can be a very lonely place. For example, the pastor can't run with the men in his church. Even with the people on his staff, he can only go so far socially. A pastor's wife cannot have women in the church as close friends. I didn't say that the pastor and his wife can't be sociable, but they can't have people in their church as "hanging buddies" because of the problems it invariably causes.

The ministry is lonely in terms of social relationships. Actually, in life in general, you can only have so many real friends that you can count on. But one thing that you're supposed to always have and be able to trust is your family. The people in your family should be your best and closest friends.

That's true in our family. As my sister said, nobody on this planet could break up our family. I don't know personally of any closer family than ours. Our family has stayed together over the years. We've never drifted apart. Our parents made the sacrifices and did everything necessary for us to be raised in the things of God. They've shown us that they love us, and they've taught us how to love each other. As a family, we are impenetrable to anything on the outside that would try to come against us.

You have to have that strong family bond if your family is to survive, much less thrive, in the ministry. As a family, if we lost every friend we have outside the family, we'd survive. We'd do just fine because we have each other, and that's all we really need.

MiChelle Butler: When the world is putting pressure on you, you need a place you can go to find rest and protection, and people you can turn to, to find love, acceptance, and encouragement.

God desires that each one of us have family relationships that are happy, healthy, and enriching in every way — spiritually, emotionally, intellectually, and socially. When a family's priorities are aligned with God's value system, they can be assured of a blessed home life, and each family member can go out and face life's challenges with confidence and successfully fulfill his or her calling.

Chapter 7
For PKs in Ministry
Part 1

Rev. Keith Butler II and Min. MiChelle Butler

MiChelle Butler: The challenges we've been talking about can be harmful to a minister's entire family, but they are usually the most detrimental to the children in the family, the PKs. As I said, children don't have as much maturity and experience to "face up" against pressure. They won't usually comprehend situations enough to say, "This is from the devil" or "What does the Word say about this?" If these challenges aren't overcome properly using godly wisdom, they can affect the PK even in adulthood.

That brings us to the sixth challenge PKs face, especially PKs who grow up and enter full-time ministry, and that is the challenge of retaining honor *God's* way when others try to *dis*honor you.

Challenge Number Six:
Retaining Honor God's Way
When Others Try to *Dis*honor You

Let's read some words from Jesus Himself along this line.

JOHN 5:41
41 I receive not honour from men.

JOHN 5:41 (*Amplified*)
**41 I receive no glory from men [I crave no human honor, I
look for no mortal fame].**

When a PK grows up and has some life experiences behind
him, he needs to learn to be sober and vigilant, as the Bible
instructs (1 Peter 5:8), because Satan is going to continue to come
against him. One lie the enemy will use against the PK in
ministry is that he or she has to be better than good in the
ministry to have any respect. The devil will try to harass and
torment PKs in ministry with thoughts of their own
worthlessness apart from their parents' ministry and calling. If
they believe the lie and act on it, it could them to get out of their
place, out of the anointing that God has placed on *them* for
ministry.

A PK in the ministry has to have his roots established solidly
in God in order to make it. He may deal daily with the thought
that others may never see him as anything else besides So-and-
so's child. A PK has to be so "tough" in God that others can't
shake his feelings of value and self-respect.

The devil will constantly put in your ear the lie that people
don't respect you for who you are. Even though you may work
very hard and go through all kinds of adversity just to hang in
there and fulfill the will of God, it's true that not everyone will
respect you as an individual and the unique ministry office God
has called you to. But you have to disregard that fact and refuse
to be distracted from fulfilling all of the will of God for your life.

A PK may study more and work harder than the next
minister who's not a PK and still may not receive the respect
that's due him. Others, even colleagues, might say, "Your position
was *given* to you. God had nothing to do with it. You're just
grabbing your dad's sermons and reading them.

Believe me, this happens, and the enemy is behind it to try to tear the church or ministry apart and wreak havoc in the lives of the people who are looking to that ministry for spiritual nurturing. Satan wants to destroy the PK's ministry and hurt the lives of as many others as possible in the process.

Keith Butler II: MiChelle and I attend certain ministers' conferences, and at those conferences, most people do not see us for who we are, ministers of the Gospel. They see us only as Bishop and Mrs. Butler's "kids" even though we are adults.

We are more than the Butlers' children. God is using us. But the enemy will use what others think to try to discourage us and hinder us in the ministry. As my sister said, it takes a deep root system to be able to be strong in the face of disrespect.

There is a certain older, seasoned minister who doesn't look at me like I'm some kid. He stands out in my mind, because not many ministers show me respect as a minister of the Gospel. Some won't even acknowledge that I'm a minister!

But when this particular seasoned minister comes to our church, he looks me in the eye and calls me Pastor Butler. I never asked him to do that; he just does it. He sees what God is doing in the church. I love to be around this man of God, because I can be myself without sensing disapproval or condescension. He doesn't judge or criticize me, scrutinizing my every move. It's a breath of fresh air to be around him and ministers like him.

What is difficult, yet not impossible, to overcome is the thought that as a PK and a minister, you may *never* cast off what I call the "shadow syndrome" — the mentality of some people who will always see you only as So-and-so's son or daughter. In other words, if you're obeying God's call to the ministry, you're going to live in that shadow for the rest of your life. And if you're *dis*obeying to try and get out of that shadow, so to speak, you're going to live in another kind of shadow that's even worse — the dark shadow of knowing that your life will never be as fruitful and meaningful as if you had obeyed God.

A PK who is a minister must get to the place where the respect or credit that's due him isn't important when it's not given. Those things can't matter to him if he's going to stay focused and do everything God wants Him to do.

MiChelle Butler: A meaningful verse to me personally is our text, John 5:41, in which Jesus says, *"I receive not honour from men."* When I first read this verse as a minister, I thought, *Man, I'm in good company!* Since Jesus could minister without the honor and respect of others around Him, I know that I can, too, because I'm doing my heavenly Father's will, and my honor comes from *Him.*

Keith Butler II: *The Amplified Bible* says, "...I crave no human honor, I look for no mortal fame" (John 5:41). The Bible also talks about not being vainglorious (Gal. 5:26). Since we are not looking for honor from men, it doesn't matter whether we're ministers who happen to be PKs or ministers who *aren't* PKs.

A PK in the ministry will have to get straight in his heart that he wasn't put here on earth to please people. He is here to please God, and while it's true that people may never recognize what you do, God recognizes it, and that's all that matters.

People see my sister and me where we are today and think that what we have was just handed to us. They don't see the hard work, the many hours of prayer and study, and the dedication and commitment to God, even through the tears, to obey Him no matter what. While the anointing *is* affected — can be increased — by association and environment, the anointing for ministry doesn't just fall on someone because of his daddy. The PK has a part to play too.

People may begin to think the same thing about my youngest sister Kristina, because she's a little dynamo who's going places! They may think that, despite her accomplishments, her success has been handed to her. But she'll make it through. I'm very impressed with Kristina, not just because she's my sister, but because I see a maturity in her already that is beyond what I was walking in when I was her age. She has a vision for her future, and she's focused and determined to take hold of it despite the challenges that lie ahead.

It is a fact that you can't control people and make them do what you want them to do or even what is right. But you can control how you react to them. The devil will put pressure on you through people and come at you hard to try to get you to react in the wrong way.

I think it's especially hard for men, because a man tends more so to identify his self-worth with his level of success in his vocation. In other words, it's a hard thing for him to face that no matter how old he is or how much he does for God, some people will not notice or acknowledge it. They won't let him stand on his own merits, so to speak. They'll only see him in light of his father and what *his father* has accomplished for God.

I don't mean to sound negative. There will be those who will acknowledge that God is working through a PK's ministry. But the devil will work overtime trying to get that PK to focus on those who criticize and persecute him.

I talked about it previously, but to thrive in the ministry, you have to get free from people. You can't be a people-pleaser and a God-pleaser at the same time. If you're concerned about what people think of you, you're on the wrong track, and you need to change. The ministry is not about being known or loved by people; it's about causing people to know and love Jesus.

Challenge Number Seven:
Striving for Excellence When You're Tempted To 'Coast'

MiChelle Butler: With the attitude in mind that you're going to please God and seek *His* honor, make sure that you work hard in the ministry. Be sure to spend personal time with God, developing your relationship with Him. Stay in the Word and be a doer of the Word. As a PK, be a model of what a minister should be.

While your position isn't, or shouldn't be, just handed to you, some things will come a lot easier to you than they will for others. But that doesn't mean that you're to sit back and relax and have the mentality that everything is supposed to be handed to you on a plate! Your attitude shouldn't be, *If something goes wrong, I'll call my daddy. He'll fix it for me.*

No, at some point, you're going to have to realize that the anointing and grace that's on your life came from God. So you need to do what is necessary to stay pleasing unto *Him*. It's God who ultimately causes you to succeed, not your daddy. And remember, if you're staying in the same place spiritually, you're not growing personally, and that's not pleasing to God. God is a God of increase.

Keith Butler II: There are two sides to being a preacher's kid — the "cursing" side and the blessing side! There are blessings you will receive, opportunities you will have, and many good things you will enjoy because of your parents. And that's not wrong. In fact, it's good, and it's thoroughly scriptural. For example, if your father is a "Psalm 112 man" and riches and honor are in his house, then riches and honor will be in your life, too, because you are his seed (v. 2). People will come against you because of that (that's the negative side), but you will experience a degree of blessing just because of who your parents are. And that's the way God wants it.

You see, as long as I'm developing my own relationship with God and being led by His Spirit, I don't mind being blessed because of my father. One of the negatives of being a PK in ministry is that he could "get by" preaching his parents' sermons without getting any revelation knowledge for himself. I believe that is the reason God didn't let me preach any of my father's sermons for the longest time. Now there's nothing wrong with preaching your father's messages. I'm just telling you what the Holy Ghost did with me.

Later, I did preach a few of my father's messages. But, at first, though some of what I preached was probably something he'd ministered before, I would not preach his messages. And when I did finally preach something he'd ministered, I didn't do it the way he'd done it. Why? Because I needed to get my own revelation of the Word. I knew my ministry couldn't consist of only capitalizing on what he'd received from the Lord.

Something that bothers me is watching a preacher's kid get up to minister without any revelation of his own. He preaches Daddy's message the way Daddy preaches it, and nothing happens. Why? *Because you* cannot effectively deliver what *you* did *not receive.*

You have to put time in with the Word for yourself. If you're going to preach another minister's message, you need to meditate on the scriptures for yourself. Put in time in prayer as he did. Seek the Lord for yourself and be led by the Holy Ghost. If you don't put the time into the message that the other minister put into it, you're not going to get the same results, and you may even get no results. You may "fall flat on your face."

On the day you stand before God, you're not going to stand there as a PK with your dad and your mom. You're going to stand before God for yourself. You, not your parents, are responsible for your future. You shouldn't be someone who just slacks off because your daddy has already built the ministry. If you have that attitude, you will eventually wreck what your father built. I've seen that happen.

We've also seen just the opposite. For example, Rev. John Osteen built a great ministry by the Holy Ghost and his years of faithful, obedient service to God. When Rev. Osteen passed on, his son Joel immediately began to take his dad's ministry to the next level. He immediately began to build on what his father had done. He could do that because he had a relationship with God for himself.

Preacher's kids must receive revelation for themselves. They must obey the Word of God for themselves. They must receive the things of God from the inside out, just as those before them did. The things of God aren't received by osmosis. In other words, they don't come from the outside in; they come from the inside out.

Serving God Is Something Worth Doing Right!

Michelle Butler: We read previously Psalm 112:3, which says about the person who fears God, *"Wealth and riches shall be in his house: and his righteousness endureth for ever."*

Let's read that verse in its context.

PSALM 112:1-3
1 Praise ye the Lord. Blessed is the man that feareth the Lord, that delighteth greatly in his commandments.
2 His seed shall be mighty upon earth: the generation of the upright shall be blessed.

**3 Wealth and riches shall be in his house: and his righteousness
endureth for ever.**

There is a saying that goes, "If it's worth doing, it's worth
doing right." Applying that to ministry, the work of the ministry
is worth putting your heart and soul into. It's worth it to be able
to stand before God and hear Him say, "Well done, thou good and
faithful servant" instead of hearing that you only partially
fulfilled your calling because you were just riding on your father's
coattails, so to speak.

It's worth it to work with all your might to accomplish that
which God has given *you* to do. It's worth it to enter the ministry
as God calls you and to obey Him yourself for your sake and the
sake of your own children — so that your seed can be mighty
upon the earth (Ps. 112:2).

You see, my dad is a Psalm 112 man, and I am his seed. If I
will just stay hooked up with God, I'm guaranteed to be mighty
in the earth for God, and I'll be able to find myself in the Bible.
I'll be able to say, "Do you want to know about me and my family?
Just look at Psalm 112 where it says that the seed of the man
who fears God will be mighty in the earth. Because my father
fears the Lord and has taught me the Word so that *I* might
reverence the Lord, I am mighty in the earth, and my own seed
shall be mighty in the earth!"

I want to pass this legacy on to my children. I want to
continue the cycle of blessing. As far as I'm concerned, every child
that comes from this line is going to be mighty on the earth,
because each one is going to fear the Lord. My children are going
to be motivated to spend time with the Word.

Fearing the Lord is worth doing. For me, it's worth doing in
order to be grown and still be in good relationship with my
parents and with the ministry. You see, in the ministry, you have

to find people to work with that you can trust. Sometimes that's hard to do, but it's a blessing when you can work with your children. It's a blessing when your children grow up to love God and want to serve Him wholeheartedly. I believe God designed it that way — so that ministers can pass the baton, so to speak, to their children and trust that they will build on their vision and continue to see it come to pass.

In our family, we all have the same vision God gave my father. We share his vision, but because of our unique personalities, we bring different aspects of that vision to the table. Yet each part fits together like a piece of a puzzle.

Keith Butler II: You can see this point illustrated as my sister and I share the message contained in this book. We are very different, yet we are alike. We minister differently, yet we are saying the same thing. The Holy Ghost uses her to touch on certain aspects of our teaching, and He uses me to touch on other things. It's a team effort.

Remaining Steady in an Unsteady World

MiChelle Butler: I especially like Psalm 1:1-3 because it paints a vivid picture of someone who's steadfast and of the blessings and benefits of being established in God.

PSALM 1:1-3
1 Blessed is the man that walketh not in the counsel of the ungodly, nor standeth in the way of sinners, nor sitteth in the seat of the scornful.
2 But his delight is in the law of the Lord; and in his law doth he meditate day and night.
3 And he shall be like a tree planted by the rivers of water, that bringeth forth his fruit in his season; his leaf also shall not wither; and whatsoever he doeth shall prosper.

Verses 1 and 2 talk about how to be established. Verse 3 talks about the blessings of the man or woman who has become established in God.

The first part of verse 3 says, *"And he shall be like a tree planted by the rivers of water...."* I'm sure you know that you can't just pluck up a tree. Pressure can't blow it down, because it's deeply rooted in the ground.

The rest of verse 3 says, *"...that bringeth forth his fruit* [not his *father's* fruit] *in his season; his leaf also shall not wither; and whatsoever he doeth shall prosper."*

Everybody wants security. Everybody wants to know, "Is everything going to be all right?" Well, as long as you stay hooked up with God, and do it right, you've got that security in Him. Even if you miss it, He'll get you right back on track and then act as if you never missed it. He will even help you make up for the time you lost disobeying Him. He has the ability to restore you and take you beyond where you were before. That's security, and it comes from God. Your confidence, your security, your vision, and your purpose lie in Him.

People are always searching for the keys to success, but true success is found in God. Success is found in fearing the Lord and obeying God — being moved by His thoughts and opinions instead of by the opinions of man. And godly success will always prove itself. It will manifest itself in ways that everyone can see and be blessed by. The success that God gives can raise up a PK to minister to some of the same people who pressured the PK as a child, and use that preacher's kid to bless and change their lives! There's no greater glory than to be able to be used by God to be a blessing to His people.

Keith Butler II: Everyone wins when you do things God's way. God's plan is the only plan that comes stamped, "Satisfaction

Guaranteed." When you do things His way, you have a guarantee from Heaven that you'll be blessed, your children will be blessed, and countless others will be blessed by your obedience to Him. You'll be a Psalm 1 and Psalm 112 man or woman! Whatever you put your hand to will prosper, and your children will get in on the blessing too!

SECTION III

Chapter 8
For PKs in Ministry Part 2 (Five Keys to Taking it To the Next Level)

Rev. Keith Butler II

It's not a foreign idea for one generation to do more than the previous generation did. That's what the world expects, isn't it? For example, in the area of technology, you enjoy the inventions and innovations of the day, but you look forward with great expectations to the next generation of technology.

For example, ten years ago, video games such as Nintendo© were great fun. But now, similar games have evolved so much that when you play one, you feel like you're virtually in the game! What happened? There was an increase. The next generation of video games was better.

Many of us have heard of the Ford family, the leaders of Ford Motor Company. William Clay Ford is the eldest, and his son is starting to take over some of the operation. It is expected of his son to make more money by the day's standards than William Clay Ford did.

The world thinks that every generation should do better. That's how God thinks also. God wants His Church to increase — to go to the next level and to *keep* going from glory to glory until Jesus returns. Now we have to find out how to do it.

Step One: Service

Let's look at what Elisha did to take what his spiritual father, Elijah, did to the next level. He served the man of God.

> **1 KINGS 19:19**
> **19 So he departed thence, and found Elisha the son of Shaphat, who was plowing with twelve yoke of oxen before him, and he with the twelfth: and ELIJAH PASSED BY HIM, AND CAST HIS MANTLE UPON HIM.**

When Elijah passed by Elisha, he put his mantle upon him. In other words, the prophet's anointing that was on Elijah was placed on Elisha. Elisha then had the anointing to be prophet.

Then we read in verse 21, ". . . *Then he* [Elisha] *arose, and went after Elijah, and ministered unto him.*" The word "ministered" means *served*. Elisha was already anointed to be prophet, but he continued to serve Elijah for quite awhile.

What's the number-one key to taking the work of God to the next level? *Serving the man of God.* Whatever mentor God has placed in your life, serve him. Be someone of service. You have to have a servant's heart to take God's plans and purposes to the next level.

Although Elisha was a prophet, during the time he served Elijah, he wasn't known as a prophet. He was known as a servant.

> **2 KINGS 3:11**
> **11 But Jehoshaphat said, Is there not here a prophet of the Lord, that we may enquire of the Lord by him? And one of the king of Israel's servants answered and said, Here is ELISHA THE SON OF SHAPHAT, WHICH POURED WATER ON THE HANDS OF ELIJAH.**

Elisha was known as the man who poured water on Elijah's hands. You may think, *I don't want to be known as that.* Yes, you do. You don't just want to be known as a great man of God. You want to be known as a servant first. If there's anything you want people to know about you, it's that you have a servant's heart. When people say that about you, you have just received one of the greatest compliments you'll ever receive in this life.

Joshua is another example of someone who had a servant's heart. Joshua was referred to as Moses' minister or servant. All those years in the wilderness, Joshua was Moses' servant. Joshua didn't preach or lay hands on the sick. No, he did the laundry, cleaned up messes, and delivered messages.

Many ministers can't handle that. And that's why they don't go anywhere. They can't handle being a servant first.

When I am in Detroit around Bishop Butler, I make sure that I pick up his briefcase and that I open the door. Why? Because I am a servant first, and I intend to stay a servant no matter how successful I become in the ministry. One of the best things anyone can ever say about you is that you're a servant — that you're interested in serving people and serving God. True leaders have the heart of a servant.

Being a servant is one of the best things you can do to fulfill the call of God on your life. He that is greatest in the Kingdom of God is the one who will get on his knees to be a servant, who will wash the feet of the person next to him, who will keep his heart pure before God, and who will humble himself (Matt. 23:11; Luke 22:26).

Make sure that no matter how old you get, how successful you become, how rich God makes you, how healed you are, or how great everything goes in your life, you continue to give all the credit to God. It wasn't by your hand that all these good things happened to you. Be a servant not only of God, but of all those around you!

God Saw a Giant-Killer in a Shepherd Boy

Let's look at the life of David, a true servant of God and man.

> **1 SAMUEL 17:1-7**
> **1 Now the Philistines gathered together their armies to battle, and were gathered together at Shochoh, which belongeth to Judah, and pitched between Shochoh and Azekah, in Ephesdammim.**
> **2 And Saul and the men of Israel were gathered together, and pitched by the valley of Elah, and set the battle in array against the Philistines.**
> **3 And the Philistines stood on a mountain on the one side, and Israel stood on a mountain on the other side: and there was a valley between them.**
> **4 And there went out a champion out of the camp of the Philistines, named Goliath, of Gath, whose height was six cubits and a span.**
> **5 And he had a helmet of brass upon his head, and he was armed with a coat of mail; and the weight of the coat was five thousand shekels of brass.**
> **6 And he had greaves of brass upon his legs, and a target of brass between his shoulders.**
> **7 And the staff of his spear was like a weaver's beam; and his spear's head weighed six hundred shekels of iron: and one bearing a shield went before him.**

This guy Goliath was massive! He was probably close to ten feet tall. He was clothed with a coat of mail, or metal, and he had a helmet of brass on his head. Then he had "greaves of brass" on his legs and a "target of brass" between his shoulders. His spear was so big that the tip of it was extremely heavy — "like a weaver's beam" (v. 7). Then he had a guy who went before him to carry his shield.

Let's continue reading in this passage.

1 SAMUEL 17:8,9
8 And he stood and cried unto the armies of Israel, and said unto them, Why are ye come out to set your battle in array? am not I a Philistine, and ye servants to Saul? choose you a man for you, and let him come down to me.
9 If he be able to fight with me, and to kill me, then will we be your servants: but if I prevail against him, and kill him, then shall ye be our servants, and serve us.

This big guy said, "I will fight one man. Whichever one of us wins will win the battle, and the army on the losing side will become the slaves of the winner's side." When Saul and all Israel heard these words, they were dismayed and greatly afraid (1 Sam. 17:11). Verse 24 of First Samuel 17 says, *"And all the men of Israel, when they saw the man* [Goliath], *fled from him, and were sore afraid."*

How many of Israel's men fled? *All of them!*

So the nation of Israel had a giant standing in their way — a giant that was preventing them from having victory. They were in a bad position, because they didn't have any giant-killers.

But God set one young man in the camp — a little red-headed boy named David, who was of fair countenance (1 Sam. 17:42). David had heard that Goliath was talking against the armies of God, and he decided to face the giant himself, because he believed that God would help him win. So he went out against Goliath and killed him (vv. 49-51).

David was the giant-killer God was looking for. And I believe God sought for him from among those who *served.* David was God's champion, but before He became a champion, he was a servant. He worked for his father, shepherding his flocks. That's where his champion's heart was developed — in his *service*, not in any great exploits that he did.

More Giant-Killers in Israel

Now David was the only giant-killer in Israel at that time. But over the course of time, David became a military legend, because he won battle after battle and war after war. He became the king of Israel and found himself again in a situation against the Philistines.

2 SAMUEL 21:15-21

15 Moreover the Philistines had yet war again with Israel; and David went down, and his servants with him, and fought against the Philistines: and David waxed faint.

16 And Ishbibenob, which was of the sons of the giant, the weight of whose spear weighed three hundred shekels of brass in weight, he being girded with a new sword, thought to have slain David.

17 But Abishai the son of Zeruiah succoured him, and smote the Philistine, and killed him. Then the men of David sware unto him, saying, Thou shalt go no more out with us to battle, that thou quench not the light of Israel.

18 And it came to pass after this, that there was again a battle with the Philistines at Gob: then Sibbechai the Hushathite slew Saph, which was of the sons of the giant.

19 And there was again a battle in Gob with the Philistines, where Elhanan the son of Jaareoregim, a Bethlehemite, slew the brother of Goliath the Gittite, the staff of whose spear was like a weaver's beam.

20 And there was yet a battle in Gath, where was a man of great stature, that had on every hand six fingers, and on every foot six toes, four and twenty in number; and he also was born to the giant.

21 And when he defied Israel, Jonathan the son of Shimeah the brother of David slew him.

David was much older at this point. The Philistines came out to battle, and David was accustomed to leading the army. So he got his sword and ran out to lead the army. But he couldn't run like he used to run. He was not as strong as he used to be.

So Ishbibenob, one of the sons of a Philistine giant, thought he had a chance to kill the king. He thought, *The king looks tired; he's trying to get his breath. And I've got a new sword. I'm going to slay King David. I'm going to be a hero.* But there was one problem with his thinking.

Verse 17 says that when this giant came out to kill David, one of David's men killed *him* instead. Now there were *two* giant-killers in Israel. Then we see in verses 18 and 19 that David's men killed even more giants.

Israel went from a nation with only one giant-killer to a nation with at least four other giant-killers. What happened? How did they go from a nation where everybody was running from a giant to a nation where men were running *toward* the giants? The answer is simple. David raised up giant-killers like himself. Following David's example today, *we* should be raising up giant-killers and mountain-movers!

David produced in his men the spirit of faith. By association and environment, they "caught" the spirit of faith that he had. They learned how to believe, speak, and act. They believed that God would be there on their behalf, and He was.

Learn How To Slay the Giants in Your Life

God has placed spiritual fathers in our lives that are champions in the spirit world. They are "giant-killers." They are mountain-movers (Mark 11:23). And many of them have paved the way for us to be successful in God. They have already done what was necessary to cause the giants that the devil brought against them to be defeated. And God has sent these men into our lives not only to prepare the way, but also to show us how to do the same thing for the next generation.

It's kind of like the four-minute mile that people said could never be accomplished. People said that there was no way a man could run a mile in four minutes. Scientists of the day said that the human heart couldn't take the exertion that would be necessary to run a four-minute mile. But then somebody did it. And then somebody else did it. Today, it seems that if you can't run a four-minute mile, you even don't belong on a track! One person showed that it could be done, and then everybody else followed.

David showed that it could be done, and then all those men followed. My spiritual father, Bishop Butler, has shown me how to be successful in life, how to be successful in my family, how to have healing for my body, and how to have prosperity in my finances. Although the world says that it can't be done, I've seen somebody do it. I know Bishop Butler is a giant-killer, and I'm going to follow behind him and slay some giants too!

God has raised up giant-killers in our lives to teach us. They've gone before us and have accomplished great feats for God. Now they're looking back, wanting *us* to slay some giants. But the ability to slay giants doesn't begin in the "ring" when you're toe-to-toe with your opponent. It begins in your heart. Have you been faithful, as David was, to God and to the man of God He's put you under to serve? A servant's heart is the first step in moving forward in the plan of God for your life.

Step Two: Submission

Remember, God's desire is that the next generation do better than the previous generation. And one way we do that is by serving the man of God that He has placed in our lives. Now let's look at the *second* key to taking things to the next level and being a generation that glorifies God.

How David's 'Not-So-Mighty Men' Became Mighty!

Let's look at a situation David faced as King Saul was pursuing him to take his life.

> **1 SAMUEL 22:1,2**
> **1 David therefore departed thence, and escaped to the cave Adullam: and when his brethren and all his father's house heard it, they went down thither to him.**
> **2 And every one that was in distress, and every one that was in debt, and every one that was discontented, gathered themselves unto him; and he became a captain over them: and there were with him about four hundred men.**

David was being chased by Saul, so he went to the cave of Adullam — a dark, damp cave — to hide. David's family found out where he was, so they called all their cousins and went to the cave also!

Now you know how it is when you get your whole family together. Picture the two cousins who are always fighting each other, the brother and sister who are always hanging out together but talking about everyone else, and the mama who always wants to slap someone "upside the head"! This is the kind of situation David found himself in. David was probably thinking, *Maybe I should just go let Saul kill me!*

It was bad enough that David's whole family was in the cave with him, but everybody who was there was in some kind of distress. Everybody was discontented. You know the kind of people I'm talking about — those who are always bitter and never happy. And then everybody there was in debt too. They were complaining about the fact that they didn't have any money.

So David went from being alone in the cave to being in the cave with his crazy family — people in debt, people who were discontented, people who were distressed. These people were supposed to be his army, his mighty men!

But something happened in that cave to change these men into mighty warriors. As we can see from the following passage, these men went from being discontented and in debt and distress to being David's mighty men of valor!

> **2 SAMUEL 23:8-11**
> **8   These be the names of the mighty men whom David had: The Tachmonite that sat in the seat, chief among the captains; the same was Adino the Eznite: he lift up his spear against eight hundred, whom he slew at one time.**
> **9   And after him was Eleazar the son of Dodo the Ahohite, one of the three mighty men with David, when they defied the Philistines that were there gathered together to battle, and the men of Israel were gone away:**
> **10 He arose, and smote the Philistines until his hand was weary, and his hand clave unto the sword: and the Lord wrought a great victory that day; and the people returned after him only to spoil.**
> **11 And after him was Shammah the son of Agee the Hararite. And the Philistines were gathered together into a troop, where was a piece of ground full of lentiles: and the people fled from the Philistines.**

We know that these men were among those who at first were discontented and in debt and distress. I mean, these men were messed up! They weren't men worthy of medals of honor. Some of them were probably worthy of jail! But something happened in that cave to change them into mighty men who could slay eight hundred men single-handedly and do other exploits by the hand of the Lord. What was it? First Samuel 22:2 says, "They *gathered themselves* unto David."

Submit to the Man of God and Prosper

These family members of David came and submitted themselves to the man of God. David was the captain over them. They recognized that they needed a leader and weren't afraid to admit it. They decided to submit themselves to David. Submission is the second key to taking things to the next level in God.

You cannot be a person in a position of authority if you are not first a person who is submitted to another. You cannot be a success in life if you're not submitted to someone.

These men became mighty because they submitted to the mighty man of that time, David. David became mighty because he trusted in God. And throughout their years with David, they learned things about trusting in God too. They gleaned from David's faith and learned that when God says something, it's so! They learned how to act on God's Word. They became mighty men just like David — so much so that when David got older, they said, "David, you can sit down now. We've learned the lesson well. Now let us do the fighting for you."

Let me give you a definition of the word "submit." It means *to surrender to the authority, discretion, or will of another.* When you submit, you're placing yourself in a position of accountability to someone. That person is your leader. You submit to him in his position over you. He tells you what you do and you do it.

Submission is not agreement. Many times people submit to what someone over them tells them to do because they agree with it. They'll do it because they think it's a good idea. But if the time comes when they *don't* agree with what that person tells them to do, they will find out if they are really submitted or not!

Real submission is not agreement; it's surrendering yourself to the will and the discretion of someone else. So although you don't agree with what the person says, if you have submitted yourself to that man of God, you must do what the man of God says because that's the man God has put over you.

Certainly, I'm not talking about following some man of God who has erred from the path and asks you to submit to something that is unlawful or that clearly goes against what the Bible teaches. When I talk about submission, true Bible submission, I'm talking about taking directives from a leader in the Lord who has received a call and is carrying out the vision God has given him. You submit to him, helping him to fulfill the call, whether or not you agree with the ways he thinks things should be done.

Let me give you an example. At my church, Faith Christian Center in Smyrna, Georgia, we provide premarital counseling to engaged couples. And we won't marry you there unless you attend those sessions. In premarital counseling, we cover all the bases, making sure you really know the person you're marrying and what you're doing as you make the life-changing decision concerning marriage.

Well, if you were to come to premarital counseling, and after a session or two, we told you that you weren't ready — that the money wasn't in place or that the relationship wasn't where it needed to be — we're going to find out in a hurry how submitted you are! You see, one reason people want to get married so fast is that they just can't hold out any longer. (You know what I'm talking about!)

If you were told to wait and you are submitted, then you would step back and pray about it, even if you didn't understand it. If one of us on the pastoral staff misses it, God will show us. We pray and hear from God. (That doesn't mean that you are to become spiritually lazy and let someone else get all your answers from God for you. You should be doing your own praying and hearing from God too.)

What most people do when a pastor tells them to slow down a bit is run off and get married somewhere else. Then they come back six months later saying, "Pastor, I've wrecked my life. Everything is terrible!" They want the pastor to fix it. Now the pastor walks in love, so he, of course, tries to help them. But his mind is saying, *Look, dummy, I told you not to do it in the first place!*

Submission is not agreement. It's surrendering to the will and discretion of another person. Your flesh doesn't want to let anybody be your boss, but you have to submit if you're going to be successful. You have to do it if you're going to take things to the next level.

Jonathan's Armor-Bearer — A Perfect Example of Submission

In the following passage, we can see a great example of someone submitting to the will of another.

1 SAMUEL 14:1-7
1 Now it came to pass upon a day, that Jonathan the son of Saul said unto the young man that bare his armour, Come,

and let us go over to the Philistines' garrison, that is on the
other side. But he told not his father.
2 And Saul tarried in the uttermost parts of Gibeah under a
pomegranate tree which is in Migron: and the people that
were with him were about six hundred men;
3 And Ahiah, the son of Ahitub, Ichabod's brother, the son of
Phinehas, the son of Eli, the Lord's priest in Shiloh, wearing
an ephod. And the people knew not that Jonathan was gone.
4 And between the passages, by which Jonathan sought to go
over unto the Philistines' garrison, there was a sharp rock on
the one side, and a sharp rock on the other side: and the
name of the one was Bozez, and the name of the other Seneh.
5 The forefront of the one was situate northward over against
Michmash, and the other southward over against Gibeah.
6 And Jonathan said to the young man that bare his armour,
Come, and let us go over unto the garrison of these
uncircumcised: it may be that the Lord will work for us: for
there is no restraint to the Lord to save by many or by few.
7 And his armourbearer said unto him, DO ALL THAT IS IN
THINE HEART: turn thee; behold, I AM WITH THEE
ACCORDING TO THY HEART.

Jonathan and his armor-bearer sneaked out to go spy on their
enemy, the Philistines.

This was a dangerous move that Jonathan made.

Jonathan said to his armor-bearer, "There's the Philistine
army, there's me, and there's you. Let's go over to the Philistine
army, and it *may* be that the Lord will give us the victory." At some
point, the armor-bearer had to have thought, *What if God doesn't?*

In this situation, most of us would have said, "Jonathan, you're
the man, but let's go back to Saul." But that's not what this armor-
bearer did.

The armor-bearer said to Jonathan, "Do whatever you feel is
right."

Let's read what happened next.

> **1 SAMUEL 14:8**
> 8 Then said Jonathan, Behold, we will pass over unto these men, and we will discover ourselves unto them.

It was getting worse. Not only were these two men about to attack a whole garrison of Philistines, but they were going to let the Philistines see them first! Jonathan wanted the two of them to walk boldly into the camp. The armor-bearer submitted and stayed right with Jonathan.

> **1 SAMUEL 14:9,10**
> 9 If they say thus unto us, Tarry until we come to you; then we will stand still in our place, and will not go up unto them.
> 10 But if they say thus, Come up unto us; then we will go up: for the Lord hath delivered them into our hand: and this shall be a sign unto us.

How did the armor-bearer know that the Lord would deliver the Philistines into their hands if they said, "Come up unto us" (v. 10)? The armor-bearer didn't hear anything from God himself. God didn't tell *him* that it would be a sign. No, God prompted *Jonathan* that that was what would happen. Jonathan told his armor-bearer, and the armor-bearer had to believe that Jonathan had heard from God.

What happened in the end? Jonathan and his armor-bearer took down twenty men, and the entire Philistine army that was encamped there began to turn on each other in confusion! God saved Israel, but I want you to notice how it happened. Since the armor-bearer didn't even have a sword, he had to trust Jonathan to kill the first guy that came against them so that he could get that soldiers' sword and have a weapon to fight with. The armor-bearer had to trust this man of God — not only his ability to hear from God, but also his ability to fight in battle!

The armor-bearer was truly dedicated to Jonathan, the man of God. If the man of God were to die in battle, he would die. If the man of God were wrong, he would be wrong. In essence, he said, "I'm going with you, Jonathan. Whatever you want to do, I will follow."

Jonathan's armor-bearer is a wonderful example of how you should be submitted to the man of God in your life.

Submission Means Staying Put in Tough Times

Submission isn't becoming afraid and running away as soon as things get tough; it's hanging in there and weathering the storm. David's mighty men were able to partake of David's blessings when David became king because they stayed with David when David was an outlaw in the eyes of Saul.

These men submitted to David and were obedient to him. They could have left at any time of their own accord. When David said something to them the wrong way or told them to do something they didn't agree with, they could have left, but they didn't. When David was running from place to place, trying to get away from Saul, they could have said, "I'm tired of this." But they stayed. And when David became king, these men who stayed with him were put in positions of authority within his army and kingdom.

These men were so dedicated to David that when he mentioned one time, "I'm so thirsty. Oh, what I would give for some water from that well by the gate at Bethlehem," the men went into enemy territory in Bethlehem to get him some water. They made their way through the enemy lines, got to the well, filled the water bottle up, and made their way back out (2 Samuel

23:16). They brought David the water because they were so dedicated to him. They were willing to do anything for him.

Be a Diligent Follower of Your Spiritual Father

First Corinthians 4:15 and 16 says, *"For though ye have ten thousand instructors in Christ, yet have ye not many fathers: for in Christ Jesus I have begotten you through the gospel. Wherefore I beseech you, be ye followers of me."* Paul was not talking about natural fathers here; he was talking about spiritual fathers.

Today we have many good Bible teachers — men of God who can preach the Word of God to us. We have pastors, prophets, evangelists, and apostles, but we only have one father. Don't forget who your spiritual father is.

Those men under David were followers of his. If David jumped, they jumped. If David ran, they ran. If David fought, they fought. If David sneezed, they sneezed! They watched David's every move so that they could do the same thing. They followed David as unto the Lord.

Joshua was like that toward Moses. Moses went to the tabernacle to meet with the Lord. And God came down in a pillar of a cloud while all Israel looked through the door. They saw Moses talking with the pillar of a cloud, but nobody would dare go near. Then when Moses was finished talking to God, he left the cloud, but someone was still in there. It was Joshua (Exod. 24:12-18). Everywhere Moses went Joshua went also.

Joshua thought, *I'm going to be a follower of Moses. Moses is a giant-killer. He's a mountain-mover. He's an overcomer. I want to be just like him. He's the mentor God has placed in my life. He's the one God wants me to follow after.* And that's exactly what he did. He was submitted to Moses.

Moses corrected him at times, because Joshua made mistakes just as all of us do. But Joshua's heart was right before God concerning Moses. And God used him to take the things that God wanted to do to the next level.

Listen to and Heed the Counsel Of Your Spiritual Father

Listen to the man of God that He has placed in your life. Make sure you are submitted. If you get stuck in a situation in which you don't agree, just make a little correction in your heart. If you want to take the move of God to the next level, it starts with being submitted.

One of the things that goes along with submitting to your spiritual father is learning to listen to the godly counsel he gives you. If you know anything about a natural father, you know that he loves his children. A father tells his child not to do something because he loves that child and doesn't want to see him get hurt. A mother tells her child not to touch the stove because she doesn't want him or her get hurt. That's just natural human love.

Paul said in First Corinthians 4:15 and 16, *"For though ye have ten thousand instructors in Christ, yet have ye not many fathers: for in Christ Jesus I have begotten you through the gospel. Wherefore I beseech you, be ye followers of me."* Paul was saying, "I am your father. You may have other instructors, and that's good. They may love you in the Lord, but I love you as a father. Therefore, I'm warning you because of my love toward you."

Those whom God has placed in authority over you have a love in their heart for you. When you go to your spiritual father to seek godly counsel, he will tell you what is best for you. Why? Because of the love he has for you.

You have to make a decision as a child of God that you're not just going to do what you want to do regardless of what he says. The minute you decide that you're smarter than your spiritual father, you will have turned into a "Gehazi."

In Second Kings chapter 5, we find the story of Gehazi and the mistake that he made. After Naaman was healed of leprosy, in his elation, he offered Elisha some money and clothes. Elisha said, "This is not the right time to receive the money" and sent him away.

Well, Gehazi thought he was smarter than Elisha. In so many words, he thought, *This rich man, Naaman, just offered my master all this money. Our ministry has light bills to pay, mailings to do, and plane tickets to buy! We need this money! But the man of God turned it away. He messed up. I'm going to go get some for myself.* As a result, Gehazi ended up getting leprosy.

There is a reason why God has placed people in your life. There's a reason why a pastor will tell you that a certain person is not the right one to marry or that it's just not the right time for you to marry. That's always hard advice to hear, but God will put a man of God in your life to give you that godly counsel because that is God's best for you. You have to learn to listen and not turn away from that counsel.

Being submitted means being dedicated to the man of God, listening to his advice and heeding it. That's what Paul was telling the Church in First Corinthians 4. He was telling them, "I'm your spiritual father. Listen to me; follow me. I love you. I have your best interest at heart." As you listen to your spiritual father and heed his advice, you will be successful. You will glorify God. You will take His plan to the next level.

Step Three: Have Your Own Revelation of God

The *third* key to taking the plan and purpose of God to the next level is having your own revelation of God. You can hear others talk about God and you can go to church services and hear about God yourself, but until you *know* Him for yourself — personally — you will never move on to what He has for you. You will never go higher than the generation before you.

Elisha Understood That He Was Anointed

Elisha had a revelation of God. He knew the God who was more than enough. Elisha believed that if Elijah was able to part the waters by the anointing of God, then he could do the same. He knew that the reason Elijah could do what he did was because of the anointing. And he believed that he had that anointing.

First, let's read the account of *Elijah's* parting the waters.

> **2 KINGS 2:8**
> **8 And Elijah took his mantle, and wrapped it together, and smote the waters, and they were divided hither and thither, so that they two went over on dry ground.**

Notice Elijah took his mantle, smote the water, and the water divided. Now let's read the account of when Elisha parted the same waters.

> **2 KINGS 2:13,14**
> **13 He took up also the mantle of Elijah that fell from him, and went back, and stood by the bank of Jordan;**
> **14 And he took the mantle of Elijah that fell from him, and smote the waters, and said, Where is the Lord God of Elijah?**

and when he also had smitten the waters, they parted hither and thither: and Elisha went over.

Immediately after the death of Elijah, Elisha goes back to the same river that Elijah had parted, the Jordan River, and he smote the waters and the waters parted. There are some things we can learn from Elisha — things that he knew that enabled him to have the same success in ministry that Elijah had.

The Scripture says, "Elisha took the mantle" (v. 14). God had called Elisha to something of great responsibility; God had given him a job to do. And Elisha took the mantle, or, in other words, he answered the call of God. He accepted the responsibility of fulfilling God's call for his life.

When Elisha smote the waters, he said, "Where is the Lord God of Elijah?" In the natural, we can't walk up to a river, take a stick, hit the water, yell something out, and see the waters part. But Elisha decided to strike the water and call on God, expecting God to part the waters. Why did he do that? What caused him to have such confidence that he would strike the water, yell out to God in front of others, and expect God to part the waters? *Elisha believed he was anointed.*

In Second Kings 2:9, Elisha said to Elijah, ". . . *I pray thee, let a double portion of thy spirit be upon me.*" Elisha did not have any natural evidence that he had received that anointing. Yet he still picked up the mantle and began to act like he was anointed.

One key to being successful is recognizing that you are already anointed. God's burden-removing, yoke-destroying power has already been smeared all over you! God has already added His "super" to your "natural"! You are equipped by God to do what He has called you to do!

Elisha Was Fully Confident

Another thing that caused Elisha to have such boldness was
that he knew that the God of Elijah could and would show up
when His people called on Him. When Elijah had called on God,
Elisha saw God show up. I'm sure Elijah must have told Elisha
the story about Jezebel and the prophets of Baal time and time
again! (*See* First Kings 18.)

You're probably familiar with the story. The prophets of Baal
took a dare from Elijah. Elijah said, "You build an altar, and I'll
build an altar. You call to your god, and I'll call to my God.
Whichever one answers by fire is God." So the prophets of Baal
built their altar and spent all day calling on their god. They
reached a point where Elijah was mocking them, asking them if
their god had gone out into the wilderness hunting or maybe he
was asleep. So they got on their altar and began cutting
themselves, doing everything they could to try to make their god
show up. Then Elijah turned around and said a short prayer. He
said, "Lord, I know You're God, and I know You answer prayer."
And — *bam* — God answered by fire!

I'm sure Elisha had heard that story many times. He knew
God would show up when God's man called on Him. He had seen
this happen in Elijah's ministry. Elisha knew the God of Elijah.
He had a special kind of knowledge of Him. He knew Him as a
God who anointed men, who answered prayer, who responded to
faith, and who honored obedience.

Because of Elisha's own revelation of God, he was able to part
the waters. In a sense, He took a big risk in the natural, because
the sons of the prophets standing on the other side were counting
on him to fail. They could have been saying, "Who does he think
he is? He thinks he's Elijah, but he isn't anybody. He was just
Elijah's servant. There's no way he'll ever be able to fill Elijah's

shoes. We're in big-time trouble. We need Elijah. Elisha isn't good enough."

You have to have your own revelation of God so that when others try to tell you that you're going to fail and that there's no way you can be as successful as Rev. So-and-so, you won't be intimidated. You'll act in faith anyway. And you'll get the results that Rev. So-and-so got, because you know God for yourself. Elisha acted in faith and God provided the power. But he did it, not based on Elijah's revelation, but on his own revelation of God.

You cannot live off your pastor's revelation or your spiritual father's revelation. You cannot live off someone else's revelation. You have to get it for yourself.

There are many believers who get angry when a man of God gets blessed, because they don't understand why *he's* getting blessed and *they're* not getting blessed. I can tell you why. You do not receive based on someone else's revelation. No, you receive based on how much revelation *you* have. I don't care if your whole church is rich; you will still be poor until you get your own revelation that God wants you to prosper.

How To Get Your Own Revelation of God

In First Chronicles 28, David called all the people of Israel together. He was about to die, and he wanted to give them his final instructions. Let's read what he said.

1 CHRONICLES 28:9
9 And thou, Solomon my son, know thou the God of thy father, and serve him with a perfect heart and with a willing mind: for the Lord searcheth all hearts, and understandeth all the imaginations of the thoughts: if thou seek him, he will be found of thee; but if thou forsake him, he will cast thee off for ever.

What did David tell his son Solomon? He said, "Know the God of your father. Know Him for yourself and serve Him with a perfect heart and willing mind." Notice that you need both. You have to have a good heart before God and you have to be able to say to God, "I may not want to do this, but I'm going to do it. And I'm going to like it, because You said to do it!"

Then we also find in this scripture *how* to get to know God. David told Solomon, "Seek Him; look for Him; chase after Him." *The Amplified Bible* says, "Inquiring for and of Him and requiring Him as your first and vital necessity." God must be first place in your life.

Seek after God in the Word. Meditate in the Word and get good teaching on the Word. Get in a church where the Word is being taught. Get books on the Word. Spend time in prayer before God. Every chance you get, find out something about God. If you seek God, He will show up; He will reveal Himself to you.

Be Strong and Obey God

God has chosen this generation to build His house on planet Earth — to continue building the Church of the Lord Jesus Christ. And in order for us to do that, we must be strong. Joshua chapter 1 tells us how to be strong so that we can fulfill what God has told us to do.

> **JOSHUA 1:6-8**
> **6 BE STRONG AND OF A GOOD COURAGE: for unto this people shalt thou divide for an inheritance the land, which I sware unto their fathers to give them.**
> **7 Only be thou strong and very courageous, that thou mayest observe to do according to all the law, which Moses my servant commanded thee: turn not from it to the right**

**hand or to the left, that thou mayest prosper whithersoever
thou goest.
8 This book of the law shall not depart out of thy mouth; BUT
THOU SHALT MEDITATE THEREIN DAY AND NIGHT, THAT
THOU MAYEST OBSERVE TO DO ACCORDING TO ALL
THAT IS WRITTEN THEREIN: for then thou shalt make thy
way prosperous, and then thou shalt have good success.**

God said, "Be strong and courageous so that you can do what
I tell you to do" (v. 1). Then He said in verse 8, "Get revelation so
you can do what I tell you to do." So getting revelation must have
something to do with being strong. You need a revelation from
God to fulfill the plans He has for you. If you don't know God for
yourself, you'll either never step out on the water, or you'll step
out and you'll sink.

So many believers have the mentality, *My dad has this
revelation, so I don't need it. Pastor knows how to get healing, so
if I get in a problem, I can run to him and he will get me healed.
Pastor knows how to get me out of this situation. He has the faith
to do it, so I don't have to worry about getting in faith. I'll just run
to him, and, by his faith, I'll get out.*

Some preachers' kids make this mistake. They become
ministers themselves, and instead of getting into the Word of God
and getting revelation for themselves, they just get up and
preach daddy's message. You can tell they have no revelation,
because there's no power behind it. Now when their father
preached the message, lives were changed. But the son just wants
to ride on daddy's coattails and not get any revelation for himself.
Therefore, people don't get blessed as they should.

That's why when I first started ministering, I never preached
my father's messages. There wouldn't have been anything
necessarily wrong with my doing that. But I just wanted to make
sure that I was getting revelation for myself. Many people won't

take the time to get their own revelation from God. Thus, they won't fulfill the vision God has given them. Don't be one of those people.

Step Four: Turn Away From Evil

In order to take things to the next level, it is important that the Word of God abide in you so that you can produce a good harvest — so that you can fulfill what God has called you to do and walk in the blessings He's called you to receive. However, in order for the Word of God to continue to abide in your heart, you must *protect* your heart, and one way to do that is to turn away from evil. That's the *fourth* key: *Turn away from evil.*

'The Fear of the Lord Is To Hate Evil'

Proverbs 8:13 says, *"The fear of the Lord is to hate evil. . . ."* And the Bible says in Proverbs 9 that the fear of the Lord is the beginning of wisdom. When you have wisdom as Solomon had, it will cause you to be extremely blessed. But if you want that kind of wisdom, you have to start with the fear of the Lord.

Then the rest of Proverbs 8:13 says, *". . . pride, and arrogancy, and the evil way, and the froward mouth, do I hate."* The word "hate" here mean *to detest; to have distaste for.* God did not tell us to tip-toe up to the line of evil and stop just short of crossing it. No, He said to *hate* evil. He hates it, and He wants *you* to hate it.

Most believers try their best not to walk in evil, but they don't *hate* evil. There's a difference. So they slip up every once in a while.

Have you ever heard the question, "How far can I go?" Single individuals ask that question sometimes. Why would anyone ask that question? If my job is to hate evil, then I should be running away from it. I should shun evil and the very *appearance* of evil (1 Thess. 5:22). I shouldn't see the line and wonder where good ends and evil begins.

Let's say, for example, that a family of skunks came running into your house. What would you do? I'm sure you would find the quickest exit and get out of there! You detest the smell of skunks. It's an odious smell. Because that smell is evil to you, you run from it.

Well, God says to hate evil. You should detest it. The smell of it should cause you to have problems. That's why you shouldn't go to a movie that contains a lot of sexual sin or sexually explicit material. You shouldn't even be there.

Proverbs 8:13 also mentions the froward mouth. Unbelievers who have a froward mouth are cursing, telling nasty jokes, and lying all the time. We are to hate the evil way — the world's way. Now we are not to detest the *people*; we are to detest the *sin*, because God said that the fear of the Lord is to hate evil as He hates it. If you don't hate evil, you're not going to walk in much wisdom. But when you hate evil, you will not be doing evil. You will be shunning it, and you will be open to receiving from God.

Don't Be Ignorant of Satan's Game Plan

Anytime the Word of God has been preached to you and you heard it, it has been planted in your heart. But Satan doesn't want you to have the Word in your heart, because with God's Word in your heart, you have the potential to get God's results. So what does Satan do? He has devised certain strategies and weapons to use against you to sidetrack you on your road to glory.

Any military person knows that the first rule of war is *know your enemy*. On a certain level, this is true in athletics. You have to know your opponent.

If you have ever played competitive sports — football, for example — you know the importance of going to the other team's games so that you can scout them, learn about their plays, their habits on the field, and so forth so you'll know how they'll react in certain situations. You can learn what defense they will use to try to stop you in the game and, therefore, be fully prepared to defeat them.

We're going to find out what defense the enemy, Satan, is going to use to try to stop you in your game in life so that you can defeat him every time.

First, like most anything else, there are holes in Satan's defensive plan. You have to find out where they are. You have to learn where the "land mines" are so you don't step on them. When you know the devil's strategies, you can go right around them. You can keep on doing what God wants you to do and be blessed.

Let's read about some of Satan's strategies.

> **MARK 4:14-19**
> **14 The sower soweth the word.**
> **15 And these are they by the way side, where the word is sown; but when they have heard, Satan cometh immediately, and taketh away the word that was sown in their hearts.**
> **16 And these are they likewise which are sown on stony ground; who, when they have heard the word, immediately receive it with gladness;**
> **17 And have no root in themselves, and so endure but for a time: afterward, when AFFLICTION or PERSECUTION ariseth for the word's sake, immediately they are offended.**
> **18 And these are they which are sown among thorns; such as hear the word,**

19 And the CARES OF THIS WORLD, and the DECEITFULNESS OF RICHES, and the LUSTS OF OTHER THINGS entering in, choke the word, and it becometh unfruitful.

With the *first* group, *"...they by the way side..."* (v. 15), Satan doesn't have to do anything; he just comes and gets the Word. With the *second* group, they *"...which are sown on stony ground..."* (v. 16), he has to send two things against them: *affliction* and *persecution*. But for those believers that he can't get with affliction and persecution, he sends in cares of this world, deceitfulness of riches, and lust of other things. And those who fall for this trap make up the *third* group, *"...they which are sown among thorns..."* (v. 18). The people in this group are full of anxiety or are caught up in the distractions of this world. They're always chasing after money, believing money to be the key to happiness. Or they are "lusting," having an inordinate, strong desire for other things in life.

You have the Word of God abiding in you. So Satan sends in the Navy Seals, so to speak. He sends in his "sin" team. He sends cares of this world, deceitfulness of riches, and lusts of other things to you to see if he can get them into your heart. That's how the devil's system works. (I'll talk more about these things later.)

Strategy Number One: Offenses

Mark 4:17 does not say that affliction and persecution stop a person from being successful. It says that a person becomes *offended*, and stops *himself* from being successful. Through his becoming offended, the Word fails to bear fruit in his life.

You see, what the enemy is trying to do is turn your heart away from God. When circumstances come against you — when bad things happen — the enemy's goal is to distract you so that you will become offended at God. Then you will say to God, "God, why did You let this happen? Don't You care about me?" And it's at that moment you become offended, and the Word of God is pressured out of your heart. *Offense* is the *first* strategy of the enemy to render the Word ineffective in your life.

In addition to affliction, or adverse circumstances, persecution from others can come against you. It may seem as if everyone is attacking you or scheming against you.

Notice that the purpose of afflictions and persecutions is to get you offended either at God or at man. If you get upset or let offense stay in your heart, it won't do you any good. In fact, it will hurt you. You won't go anywhere spiritually until you take care of that offense. Offense will always stop the blessings of God.

Don't Become Offended at the Man of God

Let's find out about another kind offense that will stop you from receiving God's blessing and from following God's plan for your life: *becoming offended at the man of God.*

MATTHEW 26:6-10
6   Now when Jesus was in Bethany, in the house of Simon the leper,
7   There came unto him a woman having an alabaster box of very precious ointment, and poured it on his head, as he sat at meat.
8   But when his disciples saw it, they had indignation, saying, To what purpose is this waste?
9   For this ointment might have been sold for much, and given to the poor.
10 When Jesus understood it, he said unto them, WHY TROUBLE YE THE WOMAN? FOR SHE HATH WROUGHT A GOOD WORK UPON ME.

First notice verse 6: *"Now when Jesus was in Bethany, in the house of Simon the leper."* Jesus was in Simon's house. Think of all the things that could have happened in Simon's life with the Master present at his house! But, apparently, Simon didn't receive any of them. It says he was a leper when Jesus came to his house, and, by every indication, he was a leper when Jesus left. Many times, people don't receive God's blessings, such as healing, because they don't respect the man of God or the anointing on his life.

Now notice what Jesus said in verse 10 to the disciples who became indignant at the woman who poured expensive perfume on Jesus' feet: "Why trouble this woman. She has done a good work." In other words, Jesus was saying, "Giving to the man of God is a good work."

Remember in Genesis 12 what God said to Abraham. He said, "Those who bless you, I will bless" (v. 3). The Word of God teaches us that we need to bless even the blessed if we want to have financial increase in our lives. We have to learn how to walk up to somebody who is dressed better than we are and give them money if God tells us to.

Jesus rebuked His disciples, because they had gotten mad over the fact that something was given to the man of God. Jesus said to them, "This is a good work. Leave her alone. Let it be."

Now all but one of the disciples got the message. Matthew 26:14 says, *"Then one of the twelve, called Judas Iscariot, went unto the chief priests."* Judas went and found the chief priests. *Temptation* wasn't chasing *him*; *he* went to the *temptation*!

MATTHEW 26:15,16
15 And said unto them, What will ye give me, and I will deliver him unto you? And they covenanted with him for thirty pieces of silver.
16 And from that time he sought opportunity to betray him.

Judas became offended that Jesus received that blessing. Offense will always lead to resentment, and resentment will always lead to betrayal. So another offense that you can't afford in your life is offense at the man of God.

One Man's Grand Opportunity To Become Offended

Let's look at an Old Testament account of a man named Jephthah and learn from his example.

> **JUDGES 11:1-3**
> **1 Now Jephthah the Gileadite was a mighty man of valour, and he was the son of an harlot: and Gilead begat Jephthah.**
> **2 And Gilead's wife bare him sons; and his wife's sons grew up, and THEY THRUST OUT JEPHTHAH, and said unto him, Thou shalt not inherit in our father's house; for thou art the son of a strange woman.**
> **3 Then Jephthah fled from his brethren, and dwelt in the land of Tob: and there were gathered vain men to Jephthah, and went out with him.**

Jephthah was the son of another woman whom his father shouldn't have been with. His father eventually got married and had more sons. And these sons, Jephthah's own brothers, kicked Jephthah out. He had to go to another land. He certainly had an opportunity to become offended.

Let's read what happened over the course of time.

> **JUDGES 11:4-6**
> **4 And it came to pass in process of time, that the children of Ammon made war against Israel.**

5 And it was so, that when the children of Ammon made war against Israel, THE ELDERS OF GILEAD WENT TO FETCH JEPHTHAH out of the land of Tob:
6 And they said unto Jephthah, Come, and be our captain, that we may fight with the children of Ammon.

The children of Israel ran into a problem, and they had to go and get Jephthah whom they had kicked out. Remember, this is the guy they had offended. This is the guy they had come against. And they came to him and said, "We need you to fight our battles."

I'm sure Jephthah must have thought, *Didn't you all kick me out?* But, you see, he didn't stay offended. Most of us would have said, "No! Die in your stupid battle, and I'll come back and establish my own kingdom when you get done." But Jephthah didn't do that. He didn't allow himself to stay offended.

Judges 11:29 says, *"Then THE SPIRIT OF THE LORD CAME UPON JEPHTHAH, and he passed over Gilead, and Manasseh, and passed over Mizpeh of Gilead, and from Mizpeh of Gilead he passed over unto the children of Ammon."* Jephthah remained anointed because he didn't allow himself to be offended.

The devil is after your anointing, because if you aren't anointed, you can't do what God has called you to do. The devil knows he has to get you offended so that you will lose your anointing. Jephthah didn't get offended. Instead, he kept that anointing on his life and won the battle, becoming the head of the tribe that had kicked him out.

Love: The Cure for All Offenses

Don't allow yourself to become offended at friends, family, ex-girlfriends, ex-boyfriends, teachers, co-workers, or anyone else.

Let it go. You should be walking in love all the days of your life regardless of what someone else has or hasn't done.

First Corinthians chapter 13 says that love pays no attention to a suffered wrong. Love does not seek its own. Love thinks evil of no one. It thinks the best of every person (*see* verses 4 through 8). You can look at someone who has done you wrong fifty times, and love will still cause you to think the best of him or her.

When people come against you and try to offend you and give you problems, you need to react "like water off a duck's back." You may see the offense, but you just keep on walking in love. If you don't have that type of attitude, then your faith won't work, because faith works by love (Gal. 5:6).

Strategy Number Two: Cares of the World

Offense is the first strategy of Satan that we looked at in detail. The *second* strategy the devil uses to steal the Word out of your heart is *cares of the world*. If you know anything about care and worry, you know it's not something you do with your body; worry is something of the heart. Remember, it's the Word that's been sown in your heart that Satan is after. The cares of the world is one strategy he uses to try to choke the Word out of your heart, making the Word unproductive in your life.

Being in anxiety, trying to figure things out for yourself, and "pulling your hair out" wondering if something's going to work out will stop you from getting your blessing. Worry is a sin; it is meditating on the lies of the devil and allowing him to deceive you into putting down your spiritual weapons so that you can't stand your ground and fight the good fight of faith. *You can't exercise faith and be in worry and anxiety at the same time!*

I encourage you to meditate on First Peter 5:7, which says, *"Casting all your care upon him; for he careth for you."* Let God help you solve the problems of life instead of trying to solve them in your own limited wisdom and strength. Refuse to worry; refuse to give place to Satan to steal God's Word from you.

Strategy Number Three: Deceitfulness of Riches

The *third* strategy of Satan is *deceitfulness of riches*. As with cares of the world, trusting in money — the deceitfulness of riches — is not a physical thing but, rather, something of the heart. You cannot chase after money in your heart and prosper in God's Word. The Bible talks about a young man who was deceived by riches and chased after money. His name was Gehazi.

Remember, I mentioned him in relation to submitting to the man of God. Well, Gehazi, Elisha's servant, not only did not submit to the man of God, but he also chased after money. And that got him in trouble.

Naaman, the one who dipped in the water seven times at Elisha's command and got healed, offered Elisha money. Elisha said, "No." Gehazi thought, *What in the world is wrong with my master? I don't understand what he's doing. He should make this man pay for his healing.* So Gehazi runs after Naaman and lies to him, saying that his master needs one talent of silver and two changes of clothes.

First, anytime you have to lie to get money, you already know you're in the wrong place. Because of what Gehazi did — because of his sin — the leprosy that was on Naaman came on Gehazi and his family forever. (*See* Second Kings 5:9-27). Why? He was chasing money.

You see, money is deceitful. Money will give you the appearance of being able to take care of all your problems and give you all the things you need. You think, *If I just had enough money, I could buy the house I want. If I just had enough money, I won't have any more problems.* No! Money is not the answer to your problems — *God* is.

Strategy Number Four: Lusts of Other Things

The *fourth* strategy of the devil listed in Mark chapter 4 is *lusts of other things*. And lusting, or lusts of other things, also begins in the heart.

Lust can be a subtle thing. First, Satan gives you a thought or suggestion. He brings it across your mind, and if you meditate on it, you'll end up with lust in your heart. And that will sidetrack you from the blessings of God and from what He has for you to do.

For example, the Bible talks about strange men and strange women who are sent by the devil to seek people out (*See* Proverbs 5). By strange, I mean morally loose — someone you don't belong with, someone who is not your marital partner.

Young man, there could be a strange woman who is *finer than fine* out there looking for you! She will study where you go, what you do, and how you do it. She'll study your work habits and routine. She'll know when you seem to be anointed and when you don't.

Don't allow yourself to fall prey to her through lust. She is anointed of the devil to try and stop you. And she will speak to you exactly what you want to hear. In other words, she will *flatter* you. And she knows just how to shake herself when she greets you. She is sent by the devil to sidetrack you, and if you decide to yoke up with her, even as a friend, you're as good as dead. The Bible says that her ways lead to death (Prov. 5:5).

Don't Settle for the Counterfeit

If you're single, I can tell you right now that the devil wants to sidetrack you by causing you to marry the wrong person. Don't marry a Delilah or a Judas! The enemy has a way of sending the counterfeit before the real thing shows up. He knows when you're close to getting with that person who's been sent by God. So the enemy sends someone who *appears* to be just like the person you've been believing for. He or she seems to be everything you want. But the Holy Ghost says, "No." Your mind says, "Yes, this is the one I want." And your body says, *"Oh, yes!"*

You see, the devil will send the counterfeit out ahead of you to try and get you to marry the wrong person. And what will end up happening if you marry that person is, you'll be fighting all the days of your life. You'll be fighting just to keep peace in your house.

Instead of reaching the world, you'll have to be constantly reaching your family, because every time you give your kids the Word, your spouse will tell them something else. You'll say, "Be healed in Jesus' Name." And your spouse will say, "It looks like you're getting worse." You'll say to your children, "You're wonderful, and you can do all things through Christ." Your spouse says, "You're an idiot; you'll never amount to anything in life." Then you'll say, "God has told me to do such-and-such." And your spouse will, "I'm not going anywhere!" And you can't go, because you can't leave your spouse.

What happened? God had a plan for you, but you couldn't be patient. So you ended up with the wrong person. You'd better wait for the right person. Marriage is a wonderful thing when you're married to the right person. But marriage is a terrible thing when you're married to the wrong person. It's as simple as that.

As I said, Satan will try to send a person across your path who may look like "the one," but the Holy Ghost inside you says, "No." You'd better not get involved with that person physically. That's one reason why sexual sin is so dangerous. It can cause you not to be able to hear from God clearly.

God may be trying to get a signal to you to show you which way to go, but if you get into sexual sin, your signal will be full of static. There's nothing wrong with God's signal, but you won't be receiving it clearly. You can't receive it because every time you think it's the Holy Ghost, your body says, "No, I've got to have that person." You're being led by the dictates of your flesh, and your ability to hear from God is hindered.

Don't marry someone because of your body — because of what your flesh tells you it wants. Instead, marry someone because the Holy Ghost is leading you. If you believe you've met the person God has for you, then go to your pastor for premarital counseling. And if your pastor says, "No, this is not God," do what he says. Remember, God has a plan for you. He's going to make sure you're blessed. He's not going to leave you out in the cold.

The Purpose for Dating

Dating is not something you do just so you can have fun on weekends. Hanging out and having fun is what friends of the same sex are for, unless you're in a big group of people in which there are both men and women.

Dating is for *marriage*. You aren't supposed to have a dating life. It doesn't exist in the life of the believer. Either you're single or you've met someone God wants you to have and now you're courting with the idea of working toward marriage.

If you play the dating game, you increase your chances of marrying the wrong person, because you'll let your emotions and body get caught up in your decision-making. All of us have done it. We've all been with someone we knew we shouldn't be with. But because we liked them so much and they looked so good, we didn't want to let them go.

The enemy wants to turn your heart from God. People you wrongly allow into your life could contaminate your heart. They could get you to begin thinking about them versus God.

Following after that strange woman or man, allowing the lusts of the flesh to reign in your life, will put you in a position where you will lose your honor, wealth, freedom, and life. This could happen while God had a plan all along to give you "heaven on earth." You could fall for the wrong person while, all along, God was going to bless you so abundantly and cause you to do even greater things than those who came before you. You can let a person take all that from you. But it doesn't have to happen!

My father talks about a number of ministers he knew when he was younger. Some of them, he believed, were better preachers than he was, but he was the only one who made it. Why? They all married the wrong women. They were just as anointed as he was. They should have all had churches of 16,000 people or successful worldwide ministries. But now some of them are working in department stores instead of doing what God called them to do, because they married the wrong person. Don't let that happen to you.

Solomon Didn't Guard His Heart

We talked about sins of the heart — offense, cares of the world, deceitfulness of riches, and lusts of other things — that will cause the Word that's been sown in your heart to be choked out. Because of his sin, Solomon didn't bear all the fruit that God wanted him to bear. Let's read what that sin was.

1 KINGS 11:1,2
**1 But king Solomon loved many strange women, together
with the daughter of Pharoah, women of the Moabites,
Ammonites, Edomites, Zidonians, and Hittites.**
** 2 Of the nations concerning which the Lord said unto the
children of Israel, Ye shall not go in to them, neither shall
they come in unto you: for surely THEY WILL TURN AWAY
YOUR HEART AFTER THEIR GODS: Solomon clave unto
these in love.**

Solomon's sin was lust. He had been warned about the
strange women of other lands. But Solomon thought, *Surely I can
date them and get them saved. I can run with them. I'm going to
affect them. They won't change me.*

You may have thought the same thing: *I can run with
unbelievers. I can date unbelievers. I can watch unbelievers on
television doing things I know I shouldn't be watching.* But, you
see, if they turned Solomon's heart, don't you know they'll turn
your heart also?

Let's continue reading.

1 KINGS 11:3-6
**3 And he has seven hundred wives, princesses, and three
hundred concubines: and his wives turned away his heart.**
**4 For it came to pass, when Solomon was old, that his wives
turned away his heart after other gods: and his heart was
not perfect with the Lord his God, as was the heart of David
his father.**
**5 For Solomon went after Ashtoreth the goddess of the
Zidonians, and after Milcom the abomination of the
Ammonites.**
**6 And Solomon did evil in the sight of the Lord, and went not
fully after the Lord, as did David his father.**

Solomon started out a success, but ended up a failure because his sin led to the split of the nation. And it was all because he didn't keep his heart right. His heart wasn't perfect before God. You have to do everything you can to keep your heart perfect. You can't let offense or anything that's not of love, such as envy or jealousy, get into your heart. And if you have bad motives in your heart, get those out too. Wrong motives will stop you from being successful.

Guard Your Mind and Your Heart And Give Sin No Place!

Satan tries to send these sins into your heart to choke the Word. So what are you to do? Keep your heart right by not allowing these things to enter in. And it all starts with your head! You meditate on worry; then it gets into your heart. You meditate on money; then it gets into your heart. You meditate on things you're lusting about; then they get into your heart. Satan's desire is to get these sins into your heart.

We've all dealt with thoughts and suggestions. The enemy suggested things to you in one way or another, and if you knew better, you knew how to resist them and replace those thoughts with the Word of God.

But if you meditated on those thoughts — if you thought about that man or woman all the time, if you thought about how money would solve all your problems — they got into your heart and eventually came out of your mouth. In other words, you began talking about them, giving voice to those thoughts. Before long, you were *acting* on those thoughts.

If you want to be successful in God, you can't give Satan a place in your heart. The Bible says not to give place to the devil (Eph. 4:27). According to First Peter 5:8, there are those whom the devil can devour and there are those whom he *can't* devour. You want to be one of those he can't devour. And you do that by guarding your heart and by being diligent in your thought-life. If Satan can get you to commit evil, he can hold you back from your progressing in the things of God. But if you turn away from evil, Satan will have no hold on you, and God's plans and purposes for your life will stand!

Step Five: Catch the Vision

The *fifth* and last key I'm going to discuss for being successful in God is, you have *to catch the vision*. No one can mentally put the vision in you. It must be "caught" as you attune yourself to the things of God.

Let's read what Paul said about this in the Book of Philippians.

> **PHILIPPIANS 2:19,20**
> 19 But I trust in the Lord Jesus to send Timotheus shortly unto you, that I also may be of good comfort, when I know your state.
> 20 For I have no man likeminded, who will naturally care for your state.

> **PHILIPPIANS 2:19,20** (*Amplified*)
> 19 But I hope and trust in the Lord Jesus soon to send Timothy to you, so that I may also be encouraged and cheered by learning news of you.
> 20 For I have no one like him [no one of so kindred a spirit] who will be so genuinely interested in your welfare and devoted to your interests.

Notice what Paul said. He said that Timothy was likeminded; he had a kindred spirit. His heart was like Paul's. What were the rest of the people like? Let's continue reading.

PHILIPPIANS 2:21-23
21 FOR ALL SEEK THEIR OWN, not the things which are Jesus Christ's.
22 But ye know the proof of him, that, as a son with the father, he hath served with me in the gospel.
23 Him therefore I hope to send presently, so soon as I shall see how it will go with me.

Most of the people were seeking their own vision. That happens a lot in churches today. The assistant pastor runs off to start his own church, and the church doesn't go anywhere. Many seek their own vision, but at the expense of what? It's at the expense of *God's* vision.

Timothy's heart was just like Paul's. His heart was after God's vision. Timothy caught the vision given unto Paul by God. What was that vision? Paul's job was to spread the Gospel, start works, make disciples, and help believers develop. Timothy had the same vision and lived according to that vision.

Titus Caught the Vision

Titus was another man in the Bible who caught the vision. Let's read what Paul said about him.

2 CORINTHIANS 8:16,17 (*Amplified*)
16 But thanks be to God Who planted the same earnest zeal and care for you in the heart of Titus.
17 For he not only welcomed and responded to our appeal, but was himself so keen in his enthusiasm and interest in you that he is going to you of his own accord.

As a pastor, I have love for the people in my congregation. And I know that when I'm not at my church, other ministers have the same love for the people there. So if I'm out ministering at a crusade, I'm not worried. I know that those whom I've left in charge love the people just like I do. That's what Paul was saying in this scripture. He was saying, "Titus loves you just as I love you."

And Titus was so enthusiastic that he went of his own accord unto the people. Titus caught the vision so much so that he actually caught it more than Paul did. He was so enthusiastic about it. He caught the vision God had given to Paul and ran with it. Paul's vision was to love the people, care for them, and teach and develop them. Titus ran to Corinth so that he could do those things, because he had caught the vision.

Titus was eager to help Paul, the man of God, fulfill his vision. That's our job today. It doesn't matter who you are, your job will always be to help another man fulfill his vision. In God's Kingdom, if you help another man fulfill his vision, God will not only bless you, but when the time comes, He will send you someone to help fulfill *your* vision.

Rehoboam *Didn't* Catch the Vision

In First Kings chapter 12, we see that after Solomon died, his son Rehoboam became king. Solomon's people then went to Rehoboam to ask him to lighten the taxes. Rehoboam went to his father's counselors because they knew his father's heart. They knew how his father would have reacted.

They told Rehoboam, "If you want to be a servant to people like your father was — if you want to keep the same vision that he had — then lighten the taxes." You see, Solomon had a vision of the king as being a servant — as being there for the people and taking care of the them, not being overbearing or dominating.

But then Rehoboam went to the boys he grew up with — people who knew nothing about his father's vision or his father's heart. They said, "You tell them, 'If you think my *father's* taxes were bad, wait until I get done with you!' Be overbearing. Prove that you're boss." That's what they told him to do. And Rehoboam did what they said instead of staying with his father's vision and his father's counselors. And it caused Rehoboam's kingdom to be divided.

That happens today among church people. If the pastor isn't there and the assistant pastor tells people to do something, they'll say, "Well, I want to hear it from the pastor." That's not running with the vision. You see, the assistant pastors have been placed in that position because they have the same heart as the pastor. Church people who won't cooperate with the assistant pastor haven't caught the pastor's vision.

Rehoboam set aside his father's counselors and did what his friends said to do. Consequently, he split the kingdom. All the hard work David did to bring the kingdom together and all the hard work Solomon did to make the kingdom prosperous was gone, because Rehoboam didn't catch the vision.

He forsook the vision that his father had of being a servant to the people — of being a good king with happy people. The Bible says that the Queen of Sheba came to Solomon's temple and said, "Happy are your servants" (1 Kings 10:8). It must have been Solomon's vision for his people to be happy. Solomon's vision, given to him by God, was that he wanted all men to have a prosperous life.

'Write the Vision And Make It Plain'

Moses had a vision that was given to him by God. What was that vision? The Promised Land. God and Moses always kept the vision before the people. Every time Moses spoke to Israel, he spoke to them about the land.

DEUTERONOMY 31:1-8

1 And Moses went and spake these words unto all Israel.

2 And he said unto them, I am an hundred and twenty years old this day; I can no more go out and come in: also the Lord hath said unto me, Thou shalt not go over this Jordan.

3 The Lord thy God, he will go over before thee, and he will destroy these nations from before thee, and thou shalt possess them: and Joshua, he shall go over before thee, as the Lord hath said.

4 And the Lord shall do unto them as he did to Sihon and to Og, kings of the Amorites, and unto the land of them, whom he destroyed.

5 And the Lord shall give them up before your face, that ye may do unto them according unto all the commandments which I have commanded you.

6 Be strong and of a good courage, fear not, nor be afraid of them: for the Lord thy God, he it is that doth go with thee; he will not fail thee, nor forsake thee.

7 And Moses called unto Joshua, and said unto him in the sight of all Israel, Be strong and of a good courage: for thou must go with this people unto the land which the Lord hath sworn unto their fathers to give them; and thou shalt cause them to inherit it.

8 And the Lord, he it is that doth go before thee; he will be with thee, he will not fail thee, neither forsake thee: fear not, neither be dismayed.

The Lord said in Habakkuk 2:2 for us to, ". . . *Write the vision, and make it plain upon tables, that he may run that readeth it."* The vision should be plain. It should be obvious to all. Moses made the vision plain to the people. He constantly told them about it. Then the time came for Joshua to fulfill the vision.

Joshua Caught the Vision

Joshua wasn't even around when Moses first got the vision. But Joshua caught the vision given to Moses by God. He accepted that this was God's will for the nation — to take the Promised Land, not to settle down in the wilderness.

God's vision was to fight seven nations without even an army. God's vision was to go to the Promised Land although most of the people with Joshua and Caleb were under forty years of age. God's vision was for the people to have a land of milk and honey — a land to worship God in freely. Joshua decided to catch this vision and run with it. Therefore, he was successful.

Ultimately, God's vision is to win the world to Jesus. If you are going contrary to that vision — if you are pursuing your own vision — there's a problem. The result of fulfilling God's vision is that you, as well as many other people, will have abundant life. But the result of living according to your way, or your vision, is death (Rom. 8:6).

God has given your spiritual father a vision or an assignment to fulfill. Catch that vision. Be committed to it. See it as God's vision, not man's, because it *is* God's vision. Go forth and fulfill it as God has called you to do. Not only will you be greatly blessed, but you will be a great blessing to many people![1]

---

[1] For further study on this subject, *see* Bishop Keith A. Butler's book *A Seed Will Meet Any Need.*

Chapter 9
Self-Esteem

Min. MiChelle Butler

And it shall come to pass in that day, that his burden shall be taken away from off thy shoulder, and his yoke from off thy neck, and the yoke shall be destroyed because of the anointing.

— Isaiah 10:27

Verily, verily, I say unto you, He that believeth on me, the works that I do shall he do also; and greater works than these shall he do; because I go unto my Father.

— John 14:12

In John 14:12, Jesus is doing the talking. He says, "He that believes on Me, the works that I do, he shall do also; and greater works than these shall he do." How is he that believeth on Jesus able to do these works? Yes, it's possible because Jesus went to the Father, but it's more than that. It's by the *anointing* that believers will do the greater works of Jesus.

When referring to Jesus Christ, some people think that Christ is Jesus' last name! But it's not; it's a description of Him. "Christ" means *the Anointed One and His anointing.* So if I'm going to believe on Jesus, then I have to believe that He is anointed. And I have to believe that the anointing on His life is going to remove burdens and destroy yokes in my life (Isa. 10:27).

167

Now if I know that Jesus is anointed, I know that when He walks into a room, burdens and yokes start to tremble because of the anointing on His life. They know that they are about to be dismissed!

What would cause people not to have their burdens removed and their yokes destroyed in Jesus' Presence? *Failing to recognize or esteem the anointing that was on His life.*

> **MATTHEW 13:54-58**
> **54 And when he was come into his own country, he taught them in their synagogue, insomuch that they were astonished, and said, Whence hath this man this wisdom, and these mighty works?**
> **55 Is not this the carpenter's son? is not his mother called Mary? and his brethren, James, and Joses, and Simon, and Judas?**
> **56 And his sisters, are they not all with us? Whence then hath this man all these things?**
> **57 And they were offended in him. But Jesus said unto them, A prophet is not without honour, save in his own country, and in his own house.**
> **58 And he did not many mighty works there because of their unbelief.**

I want you to notice here that when Jesus ministered God's Word to the people in His country, they were astonished. They said, "Wow! Where did He get all this wisdom?" (v. 54). But notice where their focus was: *"Is not this the carpenter's son? is not his mother called Mary? and his brethren, James, and Joses, and Simon, and Judas? And his sisters, are they not all with us? Whence then hath this man all these things?"* (vv. 55,56).

These people didn't believe in the anointing on Jesus' life because they were so familiar with Him. They recognized the anointing, but they could not receive any benefit from it because of their familiarity with Him. They focused on Jesus' natural family and background — His history in that country. And they became offended at Him when He tried to minister God's holy Word to them.

You Must Respect the Anointing In Order to Receive From It

There is a danger when you become too familiar with anointed people. It shouldn't have mattered who Jesus' parents or siblings were. All that mattered was the anointing. When it came time for the anointing on Jesus' life to bless them and do them some good, they couldn't receive it.

When I get up to minister, people shouldn't look at me as Bishop Keith Butler's daughter. They shouldn't look at me (or any minister) as black or white or male or female, because all that matters is the anointing. The anointing that's on my life needs to be respected if people expect to receive from God through me.

God didn't put me in the ministry to show me off. He put me in the ministry to use me, because I'm anointed. He anointed me, and as I minister the Word to people, burdens are removed and yokes are destroyed.

As we saw in Matthew 13, those who hear the Word — those who would be beneficiaries of the Word they hear — have a part to play too. Having burdens removed and yokes destroyed is not dependent just on the anointing; it's dependent on how you cooperate with the anointing.

1 TIMOTHY 6:12
12 Fight the good fight of faith, lay hold on eternal life, whereunto thou art also called, and hast professed a good profession before many witnesses.

I played basketball in junior high school, high school, and Bible school. I remember once in junior high, we were playing a very important game that was neck-in-neck all the way down to the wire. We were down most of the game, but made a big comeback in the fourth quarter. We ended up losing by one or two points, and people came up to us afterward and shook our hands, saying, "Good game. You fought hard." At that very moment, I decided that a fight is not a good fight unless I win.

The 'Good Fight of Faith' Is a Fight We Win!

The Word of God says to fight the good fight of faith. Well, it's not a good fight if we don't win. Win what? *Win victory in every battle by fighting the good fight of faith!*

We are in spiritual warfare; there is a battle going on. If you don't believe it, just read the Bible. It says that when the Word goes forth, faith comes, and victory comes with it, because the Word is anointed. But it also says that Satan comes immediately to steal the Word that goes forth (Mark 4:15). So God is telling us to fight the good fight of faith, meaning that we shall win.

You see, when God picked his "team," He picked good players! It wouldn't make any sense for Him to pick a team that has no skill or ability, because a team like that is going to lose. If I tried to put together a basketball team with no talent and then tried to play against a WNBA team, you would think I was a fool. Similarly, God has not set us up in life to lose, but to win. We are here by design, not by default!

Are You Hindering Your Own Success?

Many people don't see themselves as God sees them. They don't see themselves as a part of God's design to win in life's battles and to bless the lives of others. Their lack of self-esteem hinders them. It stands between them and the will of God, because it negatively influences their every decision and undermines their success.

I'm going to show you that poor self-esteem is a tool of Satan. Satan knows that if he can keep you from realizing your value to God, he can keep you from walking in victory and fulfilling God's will for your life. You won't reach your highest potential, whether in ministry or any other vocation, if you don't see yourself as God sees you and esteem yourself properly.

The Price God Paid for Us Revealed Our Value to Him

The Word of God tells us how we are to see ourselves.

1 CORINTHIANS 6:20
20 For ye are bought with a price: therefore glorify God in your body, and in your spirit, which are God's.

I want to draw your attention to the first part of that verse: *"For ye are bought with a price...."* God has bought us!

When you think of the prosperity of God, you know He has a lot of resources! I mean, anytime your streets are made of gold, you are pretty looted up! So since God has all these precious stones and metals in His possession, why couldn't He have just used a couple miles of golden highway to buy you back? Because even the gold of Heaven was not enough to purchase you. The price for your freedom was higher than that. It took the blood of Jesus to buy you. You've been bought with a great price!

I drive a brand-new car that I received from my parents for my birthday. It's a very nice car. I like it a lot. But if someone came up to me in a parking lot with a weapon and said, "Give me the car," I'd give it up; I'd give him the car.

On the other hand, if he came up to me and said, "Give me your little sister," I'd have a problem with that. That price is too high to pay. What I want you to see is, there is a vast difference between a material possession and the blood of one you love.

When Adam and Eve sinned, man fell from grace. He broke His relationship with God and entered into a relationship with Satan. Man needed to be redeemed or bought back. But to buy us back, God couldn't just give Satan material goods. He had to pay a price greater than any material substance. It took the blood of His Son Jesus to redeem us.

Did you ever stop to think about the fact that God doesn't buy junk. In other words, if you were not valuable, He would not have bought you. He would not have paid the price He paid. But First Corinthians 6:20 says, *"For ye are bought with a price: therefore glorify God in your body, and in your spirit, which are God's."*

Some Christians have problems glorifying God in their bodies because they don't feel good about themselves. They don't really realize that they were bought with a price. But God paid a price, a very high price, and He didn't get ripped off! He considered you worth the price He paid.

To illustrate this in the natural, a friend of mine and I have the exact same kind of designer shirt. We bought the shirts at different places, but the shirts are identical. We both wore the shirts one day and began talking about them. I found out that I paid $25 more for the shirt than she did! Now I liked the shirt, but I felt like I'd been ripped off because I paid too much for it!

Have you ever felt cheated or ripped off because you paid too high a price for something? Well, do you feel God got ripped off when He bought you? Was the price He paid too high? God says, "No," but how do you feel about yourself? How you feel about yourself — whether or not you see yourself in line with God's Word — will determine your success or failure in life.

Poor Self-Esteem Can Hinder
The Will of God for Your Life

Now when asked that question, most Christians would never admit it if they felt God got ripped off when He bought them. They would acknowledge that they've been bought with a great price, because they know what the Bible says. But let me bring it "down home" a bit: Have you ever felt like God was making a mistake when you found out something He'd called you to do? If God showed up today and gave you a big assignment, would you retreat to a corner, afraid that if God knew the real you, He would have given the assignment to someone else?

You will never be able to glorify God in what He's called you to do if you don't realize that you were bought with a price.

Self-esteem is so important. The definition of "esteem" is *to place value on, whether great or small.* Satan is going to attack your self-esteem, because how you value yourself is the underlying factor that determines your success or failure in life.

God Sees You as a Winner —
A Formidable Foe Against the Enemy —
In the Game of Life!

God sees you as a winner. He picked you to be on His team. Satan wouldn't attack you if you were a loser. In sports, the opposition doesn't usually concentrate its defense on a bad player.

When I played basketball at RHEMA Bible Training Center, we spent time in the locker room before a game, going over game plans. In any starting lineup, there are usually at least two really good players that are considered "go to" players. In other words, the team wants them to have the ball when it counts so that they can score points. So the opposing team tries to use an effective defense against those players to keep the other team from winning the game. The defense is not so concerned with the weaker players, because the weak players aren't going to do as much for their team.

I played both the center and forward positions. If I was going to be playing against a really good center or forward, I stepped up my defense. On the court, not only did I play good defense against my opponent, I tried to get in her head, so to speak. Every once in a while, I'd subtly give her a little bump or hold her jersey just long enough not to get penalized. What was I doing? I was trying to get her upset so I could distract her from her game. If I could get her riled and she began yelling at the refs, she would lose her concentration and her advantage.

Sometimes we played teams with a weak center or forward. I knew the girl was not a consistent scorer and was weak in making free throws. Against that kind of opponent, my approach was relaxed. If she got away from me while I was guarding her, my attitude was, *Oh, there she goes.* I let her go, because she wasn't going to do anything for her team.

In the same way that I plotted a stronger defense against a good opponent, Satan is going to come against *you* to try to get you off your game, so to speak. Why? Because you are a star player! You need to realize that fact and stop having a pity party. Satan is trying to stop you because he knows you're anointed to remove burdens and destroy yokes. He's not going to just let you have the run of the court, because he knows that if he does, you're going to score on him.

Fear: The Root of Poor Self-Esteem

I'm going to show you that low self esteem is based on fear — fear of not reaching your potential, fear of not being valued by others, fear of loneliness, fear of never finding Mr. or Mrs. Right, fear of marrying the wrong person, fear of rejection, fear of failing an assigned task, fear of missing important direction from God, and so forth. All of these notions are rooted in fear and produce more fear. They are not based on faith, and if you give place to them in your thought life, you won't be able to fight the good fight of faith.

In First Timothy 6:12, Paul did not say, "Fight the good fight of fear." No, he said, "Fight the good fight of *faith*." Faith and fear are incompatible.

Let's read something else Paul said in his second epistle to Timothy.

2 TIMOTHY 1:6,7
6 Wherefore I put thee in remembrance that thou stir up the gift of God, which is in thee by the putting on of my hands.
7 For God hath not given us the spirit of fear; but of power, and of love, and of a sound mind.

Verse 7 says that God has not given us the spirit of fear, but that He has given us the spirit of power, love, and a sound mind. From this verse, we know that Satan is trying to give us something, and God is trying to give us something. Satan wants to give you sickness, disease, poverty, lack, fear, low self-esteem, and so forth. God wants you to have His anointing, His power to prosper and to get wealth, and His grace, strength, and ability to accomplish what He has given you to do.

What are you going to do with what Satan is trying to give you, and what are you going to do with what God offers? I don't know about you, but I don't want something that God is not giving me. He has not given me fear; therefore, I don't want it. It doesn't belong to me, and I don't have to take it. And neither do you. Fear has no right to be in my life or yours. Fear does not belong in the life of the Christian.

Let me show you how fear works to undermine a believer's self-esteem. God will begin showing a believer some things about his future and about what He wants him to do for Him. But instead of rejoicing, the person begins to fret. He'll say something such as, "What if I'm not able to do it? What if I can't get the job done? What if something goes wrong?" The person could rejoice in faith that the Greater One in him will put him over and cause him to succeed. But, instead, he retreats in fear. That person is fanning the embers of poor self-esteem that Satan has started in his life.

There have been times that I've gotten a last-minute call to minister somewhere, and, once, I even got a call late the night before to minister in a large conference the next morning. Some big-name ministers were scheduled to minister in that conference. My first thought was, *Why do they want me in that lineup?* But if I had given place to that and stayed in that vein, fear would have been activated inside me instead of faith. You see, fear and the anointing don't go together, either. I want the anointing. I want to be able to give people what God wants me to give them. I can't do that if I give place to fear and a poor self-image.

I want you to see how low self-esteem can stop you and hinder the plan of God for your life. Fear has led a lot of ministers to make bad decisions that took them a long time to correct. For example, if you as a pastor are believing God for a church building, you need to stand your ground and not get in a hurry or in a panic and jump into something that God is not in.

I mean, a building could become available, and fear says, "You'd better jump on that opportunity. If you miss it, God won't be able to bless you." Then you might say, "Yes, I guess I should go ahead and buy that building. I'm not sure what the Lord is saying to me, and what if I miss it? Can I really hear the voice of the Lord?" So you buy the building despite the fact that you don't have peace in your spirit about it. And the situation winds up a disaster. Then, instead of working on developing your anointing to meet the needs of your people, you are praying and trying to get out of your problem that you put yourself in because of fear. You were afraid that you wouldn't get a better building, so you settled for less.

Poor Self-Esteem Affects Marriages, Homes, and Families

Some people get married because of fear. For example, a single woman might say, "Oh, he's all right. He loves God and has a little bit of money." She doesn't have any peace about marrying that man, but she does it anyway because she's in fear that she won't find someone else if she waits.

Other people get married quickly because of fear. They are afraid the pastor is going to "read their mail" if they attend premarital counseling. Then they become afraid that their fiancé won't want them anymore. So they want to jump into marriage quickly to try to avoid rejection. What they don't realize is, if that other person is the one God has for them, they will both be anointed to meet each other's needs and be a blessing to each other.

I believe fear is what led many to start the "women's movement." These women suffered low self-esteem and were attempting to gain self-esteem in the flesh by rejecting men. They weren't secure in God, in who God created them to be. If a man opened the door for them, they had a problem with it. Their attitude was, "What? Are you trying to say I'm weak?"

Fear leads a woman to become what I call a "rooftop woman"! The Bible says it's better to live on the corner of a house top than in a wide house with a brawling woman (Prov. 21:9; 25:24)! The Bible also says that a woman was made for the man to be a help to him (Gen. 2:18). Some women are so down on men, but if the man hadn't been here first, the woman would not have been made!

Some wives are so afraid their husband is going to miss it and mess up their lives. So, instead of trusting God and being confident in Him, in herself, and in her husband, she jumps out of her place and tries to take the lead. She tries to run things and be the head over that man, and she brings chaos to her house.

If you're a woman, don't be afraid of who you are. Be a woman. You don't have to be a man. I am a woman who happens to be a minister of the Gospel. I don't feel as if I have to be a man to be anointed. I know I'm anointed; I know God has equipped me to get the job done. But I also know my place. So when a man opens the door for me, takes my coat for me, or helps me carry something, I'm not offended. I know who I am, and I'm not afraid that I'll look weak or incapable.

When you feel as if you have to prove yourself to others, what you are saying is, what you have on your own is not good enough. You need to cherish the anointing on your life, the anointing you have as a Christian and the anointing God has placed on you to do what He has given you to do. It is the anointing on your life that makes you valuable to people. So esteem that anointing and work on what God thinks of you. Then that anointing will flow through you as it should. Remember, it's the anointing that counts. Satan is after your self-esteem because he's after your anointing.

Fear will negatively affect everything that you do. It will push you into premature marriage, premature relationships, premature business deals, and it will cause you to disobey God.

For the sake of argument, let's just say that Brother So-and-so just got finished "tearing the house down" with a dynamic message on getting rich, and you are up next to preach. The Lord has led you to deliver a message on the fear of the Lord and on living holy. If you are afraid and have low self-esteem, you won't believe in the anointing on your life, and you'll change your message. You'll say to yourself, *I have such a low-key message. People are going to think I can't preach. I've got to come up with something better.* If you act on that, you'll miss God. The anointing that would have been released by obeying God in your preaching will not be manifested.

Ministers sometimes change their preaching styles to copy some other minister they admire. They don't esteem the anointing God gave *them.* Therefore, they have a hard time esteeming themselves. If you're a preacher, you should *preach.* If you're a teacher, you should *teach.* Don't jump out of your calling. Learn to esteem the things that God gives and to shun the things He doesn't give, one of which is fear. We shouldn't want anything God did not give us.

You've Got Style!

Everyone has his or her own style. Have you ever noticed that some people are real cool. They just want to "work it" and be real laid back. Looking at the various ministry gifts, we can see as many different styles as we see ministers! One evangelist may jump and spin when he preaches. He has an exuberant style.

Another minister, a teacher, perhaps, may be reserved. But each one should minister with the style of God.

God can give a style to one that makes him appear flamboyant. To another, He gives a style that makes him appear calm and collected. God is a big God. He gives many different styles, and, while each person's style is manifested differently, he can still say he ministers with the style of God.

We are created in God's own image and likeness. Since that is true, we shouldn't want or try to be like someone else, because we should know and be confident that we are reflecting the image of God in our own individual calling. Since we're like our heavenly Father, we should know that we're equipped for the job and that we can perform it with style!

The style of God has to do with more than just mannerisms. It also has to do with attitude and perspective. For example, since we have the style of God, we should see things from His point of view, according to His Word. I should never entertain a thought that suggests I can't fulfill God's call on my life, because fear of failure is not God's style! Quitting is not my Father's style. And I should never receive the thought that I'll go broke and be broke the rest of my life, because "broke" is not God's style! It isn't God's style to be sick. It isn't His style to be ugly, and it isn't His style to be worthless! And I have His style because I was created in His likeness. God is anointed, and *I* am anointed. I have His style.

God has not provided the anointing just for those in the fivefold ministry. God has an anointing for whatever He has called you to do. At various times, members of my family have been under the care of our orthodontist, who is an *anointed* orthodontist! When you walk into his office, you can tell a difference. But what would happen if he decided to step out of his anointing because he wanted to be and do something else? The anointing that is on his life now would no longer benefit us and his other patients.

You see, the anointing on your life is not just for you. We are here to bless each other.

How To Build Your Self-Esteem With the Word of God

Many people have identified the fact that they suffer from low self-esteem. But once you recognize the problem, how do you go about fixing it? First, you have to have revelation knowledge — heart knowledge, not just head knowledge — of how God sees you. You can't learn to esteem yourself properly without understanding how God esteems you.

Let's look at the creation of man as recorded in the Book of Beginnings to see how God sees us.

> **GENESIS 1:26**
> **26 And God said, Let us make man in our image, after our likeness: and let them have dominion over the fish of the sea, and over the fowl of the air, and over the cattle, and over all the earth, and over every creeping thing that creepeth upon the earth.**

Notice here that it said that God made man in His image and His likeness, and gave him dominion. God created us in the image and likeness of Himself, and He created us to have dominion. Think about that! That in itself is enough to change the way we see ourselves.

The word "image" means, in effect, *a sculptured likeness*; *a copy*. Very simply, we are "carbon copies" of God!

When you talk about a person being made in the image of someone, you're talking about how that person looks or how he projects himself. Now in terms of my looks, I think I am a good mix between my mother and father. Some people tell me, "You look just like your dad." And others say, "You look just like your mom."

Well, if you like the way your parents look (and I do), you would take comments like that as a compliment. But what if someone said to you, "You're the spitting image of your mama. You look just like her. Your mama is ugly"?

That's not a compliment. That person has just told you that you're ugly, because you have your mother's likeness, and we said that when you talk about being made in the image of someone, you're talking about appearances. Well, since we are all made in the image of God, *who are we to call ourselves ugly*?

When God looks at you, He sees His likeness. And that's how you are to see yourself. Again, what is important is the anointing. The anointing does not come from the world. So if the world says a woman has to be tall and waif-like to be pretty, are you going to believe it? If you're short and plump, does that mean you're ugly? The world might say yes, but you need to say, "Says who?"

Is Your Faith in the *World* or in the *Word*?

Your worth is not based on what the world says. The problem is, so many have *allowed* their own sense of worth to be based on the opinions of the world. They need to ask themselves, "What has the world done for me? And upon whose judgment is their opinion based, anyway?"

When you allow yourself to receive negative thoughts about yourself, you are siding in with the devil and the world, and you're siding *against* God, in whose image you were made. When you say, "I can't get up in front of people because my clothes don't measure up," or "I'm too tall," "I'm too short," or "I'm not good enough," you are undermining your own self-esteem. You are insulting God's handiwork.

If you feel ugly, you need to ask yourself why you feel that way. You are made in the image of God, so if you're ugly, that means God is ugly too. Then look at the flip side of that. You can say, "God is a good God. God is a beautiful God. I am created in His image. Therefore, I am beautiful too."

Some people have a sense of worthlessness ingrained in them because they've been told their entire lives that they are worthless. Then they grow up fixated on their own weaknesses and shortcomings, and their constant attitude is, *I need to fix this and that about myself.*

I have a word for people like that — I have *the* Word, the Word of God, and the Word says something entirely different! Not only that, but the Word is anointed to remove burdens and destroy yokes (Isa. 10:27). These people just need to stay with the Word and fight the good fight of faith. They need to get in the game and fight! In a game of basketball, for example, you can't play to win if you're sitting on the bench. No, you have to get out on the court and do something. Similarly, to overcome low self-esteem, you have to hear the Word and *act on it*. And you should have fun doing it! You can have fun acting on the Word when you know you're going to get results.

We know that low self-esteem is rooted in fear, and it's evidenced by fear. A person with a poor self-image is a fearful person. There is another indication of low self-esteem, and that's *selfishness*. For example, a person with low self-esteem will say, "*I'm* not going to get my needs met," "People don't think *I'm* great," or "*I'm* not appreciated."

Notice the emphasis on "self." Another indication of low self-esteem is *comparison*. The emphasis is still on "self," but when you compare yourself with others, your "self" is the one who usually comes up short.

If you are secure in God, and you are confident in the anointing He has placed on you, you won't compare yourself with others to see how you're measuring up. If you're a minister, for example, you won't be intimidated, even by older, more experienced ministers. You'll be too busy removing burdens and destroying yokes.

You see, what matters is the anointing. Are burdens being removed and yokes destroyed? It doesn't matter which minister has the biggest auditorium. Some ministers compare how fast they acquired church property in relation to another minister who acquired property. Some try to determine if their ministry has grown sufficiently by comparing themselves to others who have been in the ministry the same length of time they have. If two ministers have been in the ministry twelve years, for example, but the second minister has a larger church, then the first minister feels his church hasn't grown enough, and he feels inferior and intimidated.

The best part about the anointing is that it crosses all borders. So if you are Caucasian and you minister to a congregation of African American folks, you have no right to be intimidated, because the anointing, not your commonality, crosses that border and removes burdens and destroys yokes.

You Are the Image and Glory of God!

First Corinthians 11:7 says, *"For a man indeed ought not to cover his head, forasmuch as he is the image and glory of God: but the woman is the glory of the man."*

The word "glory" means *majestic beauty or splendor*; *something that brings honor or renown*. So according to First Corinthians 11:7, man is not only the image of God, but His glory.

What does it mean to be God's glory? To illustrate in the natural, if you were standing in your church parking lot and saw a canary yellow Ferrari with a black top go by, what would you say? You'd probably say, "Whose is that?"

Once you found out who owned the car, you'd want to know about the person. What does he or she do for a living? Your attitude would be, *Boy, God must be showing Himself true in your life, because that is an expensive car!*

You see, in a sense, that car is somebody's glory. And because of that "glory," people began to sing his praises, and they wanted to know more about him.

You are the glory of God. When you base your self-esteem on that truth, you will be confident. Your attitude will be, *I'm God's style!* You'll be able to walk through adversity, knowing that you are created in the image and likeness of God, that you are His glory, and that you belong to Him.

Others will see it too. They'll know that there's something different about you — something good — and they'll want to find out about the One you belong to so they can praise Him. In much the same way the owner of the new Ferrari gets recognition because of His possession, God will get the recognition, honor, and glory for your life. When you're walking with confidence in your calling, respecting the anointing He has placed upon you, others will notice, because you're Somebody's glory.

I'm not telling you this just so you'll have a great self-image. Yes, God wants you to have self-esteem and a healthy self-image or sense of worth. But this isn't only about us. Not everyone who gets saved will do so inside the four walls of a church building. But you might be in the mall, for example, when someone approaches you and says, "There's something different about you. I couldn't help but notice that you're so peaceful and happy. May I talk to you for a minute?"

Right then, you have an opportunity to usher someone into the Kingdom of God. But if you're walking around looking depressed or as if you would run if someone talked to you, you are projecting to others a low self-esteem. What would you be able to tell someone who's not saved — how not to be like you?

You should feel good about the fact that you are God's glory. That should make you feel important. The value that God Himself has placed on you should be the value you place on yourself.

Do you remember in high-school that if someone of the opposite sex really liked you, you felt honored depending on who it was that liked you? For example, if someone labeled a "geek" or "nerd" valued you and paid special attention to you, you wouldn't be flattered, and you certainly wouldn't tell anyone else about it. But if the captain of the football team or one of the cheerleaders showed an interest in you, you'd be excited and you'd grab the first friend you could find so you could tell someone! Why? Because you valued the person who valued you. His or her admiration meant something to you. It made you feel important.

When a woman is given in marriage, she becomes the glory of someone else. He may be a professional basketball player or a doctor or someone else the world holds dear. Or you might be the glory of a big-name minister. But you need to realize that that man has nothing on God. To be God's glory is the greatest honor that can be bestowed. And you *are* God's glory!

The same is true for a man who marries a beautiful, talented woman. She might be Miss USA, but she doesn't have anything on God! She can't do for his self-esteem what God can do.

You are God's glory. And, remember, God owns streets of gold and untold resources. Why couldn't His streets of gold be His glory? Why did He pick you and me? Because we are created in His image and likeness, and we were bought with a price. We have His style and His anointing. When that truth really sinks in, you will feel good about yourself.

A Minister's Responsibility
To Love and Respect Himself

Did you know that there are ministers of the Gospel who have low self-esteem? But a minister who cannot love and respect himself will not be as effective or successful in the ministry as the minister who sees himself as God sees him and walks in the light of that.

Certainly, a minister can come across as having a healthy self-image when he's preaching or teaching. But what about when he or she goes home? After a minister preaches can be the loneliest time in the world. When the anointing lifts, he or she might wonder, *Did I deliver the message well enough? Did the people get it?* If a minister becomes overwrought with self-doubt, he may go home snapping at his family. He may end up hurting the self-esteem of his family members, because if a person doesn't reverence and respect the image of God on the inside of him, he won't be able to respect or value it in anyone else.

Ministers fall into the poor self-esteem trap and then keep themselves there by trying to equate their self-worth with their exploits in the ministry rather than with who they are in Christ. They lay hands on people to see a miracle because they think that is what is going to make their ministry grow. If they feel their ministry is successful, they will feel better about themselves.

But we are to lay hands on people because we love them. We lay hands on them because they're our brothers and sisters in Christ who are in need. They're bound and we know we can set them free, because the Word says, *"... they shall lay hands on the sick, and they shall recover"* (Mark 16:18).

A minister is a servant. He or she shouldn't lay hands on people for show. Love should be his motive. He should minister to others because he loves them, not because he's trying to impress anyone.

When love is your motive, you will stay on the path God has put you on. You won't stray, making bad decisions based on what someone else is doing instead of on what God has told you to do. For example, if you're buying a church building, you won't be thinking, *I can't buy this building. It's not as impressive as So-and-so's* or, *What will people think? I'm not growing as fast as such-and-such church.*

That's why it's so important that a minister learns to love and respect himself. If he can't take care of the home base, so to speak, everyone who sits under his ministry is going to fall by the wayside.

Two Keys to Happiness: Serving Others As Unto the Lord and Looking to Him, Not People, as Your Source

And let me say something else along this line: If those in the ministry are called to serve, *everyone* is called to serve, including husbands and wives! The attitude should be "what you can do for the other person," not "what the other person can do for me."

It's not another person's job to make you happy or make you feel good about yourself. You are not a "feeler" — you're not a soul — you are a spirit. You *are* a spirit, you *have* a soul, and you *live in* a body (1 Thess. 5:23). And the only thing that's going to change your spirit is the anointing, not another person.

It's good to get full in God. In other words, when He is your source, He can do in your life "exceeding abundantly above" all you can ask or think (Eph. 3:20). I call that "overflow blessing"! You can't get that looking to a person to meet your need. Ephesians 3:20 talks about *God* doing exceeding abundantly above all you can ask or think. Well, I can ask for and think of a whole lot of things — but He can do even better than that! He can do *exceeding abundantly above*!

Single person, when you meet your mate, you want to be full in God. If you haven't taken the time to learn who you are in Christ and to respect the anointing on your life, your cup, so to speak, will be half empty. Then suppose you meet that special someone. One day, he or she is filling your cup with a whole lot of water, and you're overflowing with self-esteem on that day. Then the next day, he or she may just pour in a little drop; you're still half empty. Your attitude changes, and you say something like, "You don't appreciate me."

But, you see, it wasn't that other person's job to fill your cup. You should keep your cup full in God. If your cup is full in God, it doesn't matter how much another person pours into you — whether it's a little or a lot — it's all overflow.

Hold on Tight! Satan Wants You To Let Go of Your Anointing

We need to hold on to our self-esteem and the anointing that's on our life. I want to show you through the example of Adam and Eve the consequences of letting go of your anointing.

GENESIS 3:11-15
11 And he [God] said [to Adam], ...Hast thou eaten of the tree, whereof I commanded thee that thou shouldest not eat?
12 And the man said, The woman whom thou gavest to be with me, she gave me of the tree, and I did eat.
13 And the Lord God said unto the woman, What is this that thou hast done? And the woman said, The serpent beguiled me, and I did eat.
14 And the Lord God said unto the serpent, Because thou hast done this, thou art cursed above all cattle, and above every beast of the field; upon thy belly shalt thou go, and dust shalt thou eat all the days of thy life:
15 And I will put enmity between thee and the woman, and between thy seed and her seed; it shall bruise thy head, and thou shalt bruise his heel.

When man fell, he let the anointing go. He let it go because he was disobedient to God. But even in his fallen state, man is still better than the devil. God told the serpent — the devil — even after Adam and Eve's fall, that the woman's seed would bruise his head.

The devil is nothing but a fallen angel, but human beings are made in the image and likeness of God. Angels were not created in God's image. God made man higher than the angels — greater than the devil and all his fallen cohorts.

God destroys the works of the devil through His anointing. But when Adam sinned, the anointing lifted. Yet God said that the seed of the woman was going to bruise the devil's head. That meant that somebody in the line is going to have to get the anointing back.

Satan knows the power of the anointing, because he was once anointed too.

EZEKIEL 28:12-14
12 Son of man, take up a lamentation upon the king of Tyrus, and say unto him, Thus saith the Lord God; Thou sealest up the sum, full of wisdom, and perfect in beauty.

13 Thou hast been in Eden the garden of God; every precious stone was thy covering, the sardius, topaz, and the diamond, the beryl, the onyx, and the jasper, the sapphire, the emerald, and the carbuncle, and gold: the workmanship of thy tabrets and of thy pipes was prepared in thee in the day that thou wast created.
14 Thou art the anointed cherub that covereth....

This passage was talking about the devil before his fall. When Satan sinned, he fell fast from Heaven — like lightning (Luke 10:18). God stripped him of his anointing. We just read here that he was the anointed cherub (Ezekiel 28:14). Satan knows the power of the anointing, because he was once anointed. That's why he comes to you with deception to try to rob you of your self-esteem. He knows that with the anointing you cannot be stopped.

Demons cannot stay where the anointing is unless the person who's anointed doesn't realize he's anointed. Years ago, a movie came out that featured "gremlins." In the movie, whenever these creatures got into the light, they said, "Bright light. Bright light. Bright light." Well, you as a believer walk into a room, demons says, "Bright light. Bright light. Bright light." They can't stay in the light unless you allow them to through your ignorance of God's Word. Those demons will try to stick around. They'll say, "He's anointed, but let's see if he *knows* he's anointed." Then when they hear you say, "Oh, I can't do anything," they know you're ignorant.

Satan understands the anointing. When Adam and Eve fell and God said the seed of the woman was going to bruise the serpent's head, what did the serpent do? The serpent, Satan, knew that the seed of the woman was going to have to have the anointing in order to bruise his head, so he immediately sought to destroy anyone he thought might potentially get back the anointing. We saw it with Cain and Abel. Abel was obedient to

God, so he could be the one. When it looked like Abel was about to be anointed, Satan used Cain to kill him.

Satan knows the power of the anointing, and he is afraid of it. God destroys yokes through the anointing. The works of Satan are destroyed through the anointing. Satan was looking for the person who would get the anointing back. He tried killing the prophets. He was searching for the one who'd be anointed.

But notice God Himself openly revealed who that Person was.

LUKE 3:21,22
21 Now when all the people were baptized, it came to pass, that Jesus also being baptized, and praying, the heaven was opened,
22 And the Holy Ghost descended in a bodily shape like a dove upon him, and a voice came from heaven, which said, Thou art my beloved Son; in thee I am well pleased.

After Jesus was baptized by John the Baptist, it was as if God was saying to the devil, "You don't have to look. I'm about to tell you who He is. It isn't a secret, so listen up!" Then God spoke from Heaven, saying, "This is My beloved Son. In Him I am well pleased" (v. 22).

So God let the devil know, "This is the Anointed One. This is the manifestation of what I said to you in the Garden of Eden. Your head is about to be bruised!"

So what did Satan do? He crucified Jesus. He thought that if he could kill Jesus, his head wouldn't be bruised. That was foolish thinking, because God had already said, "Your head is going to be bruised." The Word says that if the devil and demons had only known the plan of God, they would not have crucified the Lord of Glory (1 Cor. 2:8). What was the plan of God? That when Jesus Christ the Anointed One would be crucified, it would make you and me anointed too. All who would believe on Jesus' Name would receive of that anointing and become a joint-heir with Christ, sharers of His glory — the anointing.

Remember we read John 14:12, in which Jesus says, *"Verily, verily, I say unto you, He that believeth on me, the works that I do shall he do also; and greater works than these shall he do; because I go unto my Father."* Jesus' works became multiplied through His death, burial, and resurrection, because instead of only Jesus or His disciples doing the works, the entire Body of Christ can do the works! We all have received the power to become sons of God (John 1:12), so instead of one Jesus, in a sense, there are now *millions* of Jesuses!

Satan thought he'd won when he crucified Jesus, but, really, God set Satan up! I mean, Jesus bruised Satan's head when He rose from the dead. When He rose again, He rose with all power and dominion — and with the anointing of God — and He said, *"...All power is given unto me in heaven and in earth. GO YE THEREFORE, and teach all nations, baptizing them in the name of the Father, and of the Son, and of the Holy Ghost"* (Matt. 28:18,19).

You are anointed. So everything you do should be stepping on Satan. He is under your feet, and your heel bruises his head. You are anointed of God. Nothing in this world should hold you back. But it takes knowing who you are in Christ. It takes having self-esteem and a good self-image. Poor self-esteem will keep you from doing the works that Jesus did.

Jesus Esteemed Himself and The Call of God on His Life

Think about it. If Jesus had had low self-esteem, He would have never been able to say, "I am that I am" (John 18:5,6; Rev. 1:18). And if He had not said, "I am that I am," we would not be who we are.

Jesus could have bought Satan's lies. For example, Jesus did not get married, so He could have had the thoughts, *I'm thirty years old and not married. That must mean that nobody wants me.* But if He had bought into that lie, where would we be?

Jesus' life was for us, just as our life is for others. We are anointed. Therefore, we need to "get it together" and refuse to allow Satan to stop us. We are God's style. We need to follow the steps of Jesus and walk the walk. It's a sweatless anointing, because we don't have to get caught up trying to be somebody. We already are somebody in Christ! We just need to believe it.

We Are Here By Design, Not Default!

We are not living by default, but by design. I am designed to set people free. I am designed to remove burdens and destroy yokes through the anointing. I am designed to be in God's style. I am designed to be in the image and likeness of God.

Therefore, I won't live by default. I won't accept the lies of the devil that I can't do what God has called me to do. I'll never accept the lies of the devil that I can't minister to people effectively. I am anointed. I am designed. That means that Somebody took time with me. I am not a thrown-together job.

And I won't fellowship with people who continually say things that attack my self-esteem. I value the anointing that's in me and upon me to fulfill the call of God on my life. I won't take this anointing just anywhere. I'm not going to the clubs with this anointing. I'm not going to subject this anointing to fornication. I value what God has given me.

A Divine Cooperation:
Working Together With God

Someone might say, "All that sounds good for you, but I don't *feel* very anointed." But you don't walk in the anointing by your feelings; you walk in it by your faith.

ISAIAH 43:26
26 Put me in remembrance: let us plead together: declare thou, that thou mayest be justified.

The Lord says, "Put Me in remembrance. Let us plead together." I want you to think of a court room. You are on trial, and present are you, your attorney, the prosecution, and the judge.

Your attorney says, "Let us plead *together*." But in order for the two of you to plead *together*, you both have to be saying the same thing. He is there to defend you — to plead your case. But you have to be in agreement. It doesn't matter if the prosecution whispers, "Last Sunday your church attendance was down," even if it sounds true, you need to continue to side in with your defense. And he says, "You're anointed. You have everything you need right there on the inside of you."

Or the prosecution might say, "Your kids will go wild. You won't be able to raise godly offspring." You need to stay in agreement with your defense attorney. So you say what He says. You say, "God gave me those kids, and I know that I'm anointed to be more than enough of what they need. I *will* raise godly seed."

You need to shake off the feelings of low self-esteem that have come to rob you of your anointing. You may need to finish school, and a poor self-image has kept you from doing that. You may need to change jobs or move to another city, but fear and low self-esteem have hindered you. You need to shake off those feelings and go ahead and do whatever it is God has called you to do. You don't need to accept fear or anything else that God did not give you.

We know that Satan can't arbitrarily or at will do anything about your anointing. But he can try to deceive you into letting it go. If you buy into his lies, you are no longer "pleading together" with the Lord anymore. You're siding against Him, and you're siding in with the devil.

If you were in a real court room accused of some crime you didn't commit, you would have an attorney to defend you. But if *he* is building a case for you, claiming your innocence, while *you* are saying that you're guilty, you are going to have a problem. You and your attorney are on the same team, but you are working against him.

Similarly, when the devil accuses you, even if you did wrong, you need to run to the aid of your Defense. If you've asked God to forgive you, you need to say only what your Defense, Jesus the Word of God, says about you. If He says, "He's innocent. My blood has cleansed him," then you say, "I'm innocent. Jesus' blood has cleansed me."

We know that the Word of God is anointed. But in order for that anointing to work for you, you have to cooperate with it. You have to agree with God. You have to release your faith in God's Word, because you have to believe it in order to receive it.

In a court case, what is the one thing that you need to win the case? *Evidence.* Hebrews 11:1 says, "*...faith is the substance* [evidence] *of things hoped for, the evidence of things not seen.*"

As you "plead together" with God, agreeing with Him against all opposition, you are fighting the good fight of faith. And that faith in God and His Word secures your victory. You have all the evidence you need in God's Word if you'll believe. When you release your faith in the Word, that is the evidence that you present. And that evidence is acceptable to God, the Judge, and He rules in your favor, saying, "Case closed."

Chapter 10
A Tale of Three Generations

Rev. Keith Butler II

God had a land where He wanted Abraham to go — the Promised Land — and God has a land for you. There is a particular role that God has called you to fulfill. And it is important to know what that role is — what God's perfect will is for your life. God has a land for you, and He has a plan to get you to that land.

God also has a land for the Church as a whole. God has a land for this generation. All of us have a role in helping the Church fulfill God's plan. And that plan is to win the world to Jesus and to usher in His return.

Let's look at the nation of Israel and find out all the things that are right to do when following God's plan and getting to God's land. Then let's discover from their example the things that are *wrong* to do when following God's plan. God has a perfect will and plan for everyone. God has an end result that He wants to see in your life, just like He had an end result that He wanted to see in Abraham's life.

God's Perfect Will for Abraham

What was God's perfect will for Abraham?

GENESIS 12:1-3
1 Now the Lord had said unto Abram, Get thee out of thy country, and from thy kindred, and from thy father's house, unto A LAND THAT I WILL SHEW THEE:

2 And I will make of thee a great nation, and I will bless thee, and make thy name great; and thou shalt be a blessing: 3 And I will bless them that bless thee, and curse him that curseth thee: and in thee shall all families of the earth be blessed.

God gave Abraham a directive. He gave him an order to leave his family, his kindred, his country, and to go to a land that God would tell him about in the future. What God laid out in these three verses was His perfect will for Abraham's life.

God's perfect will for Abraham was not to stay with his parents or even stay in his country. God's will was for him to go to a particular place, do a particular thing, and have a particular result in his life. As I said, God's perfect will for Abraham was the Promised Land. Abraham's obedience to go there would have far-reaching results. It would make him the father of many nations, the patriarch through which the Seed, the Lord Jesus Christ, would come, and the father of our faith today.

Although God had a perfect will for Abraham, that didn't mean that Abraham was just automatically going to walk in it. Abraham is often referred to as the "father of faith," but he still messed up at times. God told him to leave his family and go to a land. Abraham left, but he brought his cousin Lot with him! Abraham left his father's house, but he brought his cousin and ended up going on a detour.

Have you ever taken a detour on the road of God's plan? God told you to do something and you got scared and did something else, or you only did *half* of what God said. That detour wasn't any fun, but even though you may have messed up, God can still turn it around when you get it right.

Abraham went to Egypt with his cousin Lot. But as soon as Abraham corrected things, Lot left him, and Abraham got to where God wanted him to be. Then God said, "All right, My promise for you is still so."

Let's read what God said to Abraham after he corrected things.

> **GENESIS 13:14-16**
> **14 And the Lord said unto Abram, after that Lot was separated from him, Lift up now thine eyes, and look from the place where thou art northward, and southward, and eastward, and westward:**
> **15 For all the land which thou seest, to thee will I give it, and to thy seed for ever.**
> **16 And I will make thy seed as the dust of the earth: so that if a man can number the dust of the earth, then shall thy seed also be numbered.**

God had a perfect will for Abraham's life — to get to that promised land. Abraham's end result was that he would be blessed, that his name would be great, and that through him all the nations of the earth would be blessed. These are the things that were supposed to happen by the end of Abraham's life. After his death, these were the things that were supposed to be said about Abraham. And we know that Abraham did fulfill God's perfect will.

God's Perfect Will for You

God has a perfect will for your life. And when God looks at you, He sees the end from the beginning. God's not looking at your failures or where you've messed up. God is looking at the end result — what you will be. So He's doing His best to get that to manifest or come to pass in the natural, because He already sees it in the spirit realm.

The main way to find out God's will for your life is in prayer. But even after you find out that plan and say, "Yes, Lord," the devil is still going to try to stop you from fulfilling that plan.

You might obey God, step out in faith, and leave for your land as Abraham did, but the devil will step up his attack against you, because he does not want you to fulfill God's perfect will for your life. He knows that if you get God's perfect will for your life, not only will you have "heaven on earth," but you'll end up bringing "heaven on earth" to the lives of many others.

In order for God's will to come to pass in your life, there are certain things you have to do and other things you have to avoid. Let's learn from the nation of Israel what they did and didn't do.

The First Generation Escaped The Bondage of Egypt

In looking at the nation of Israel, we're going to start with the first generation. The first generation had the faith to get out of Egypt.

Let's read about this first generation in Psalm 105.

> **PSALM 105:37-44**
> **37 He brought them forth also with silver and gold: and there was not one feeble person among their tribes.**
> **38 Egypt was glad when they departed: for the fear of them fell upon them.**
> **39 He spread a cloud for a covering; and fire to give light in the night.**
> **40 The people asked, and he brought quails, and satisfied them with the bread of heaven.**
> **41 He opened the rock, and the waters gushed out; they ran in the dry places like a river.**

42 For he remembered his holy promise, and Abraham his servant.
43 And he brought forth his people with joy, and his chosen with gladness:
44 And gave them the lands of the heathen: and they inherited the labour of the people.

God brought the children of Israel out of Egypt with silver and gold and healing — divine prosperity and health. But then notice verse 44: *"And gave them the lands of the heathen: and they inherited the labour of the people."* Who were the "them" and the "they" in that verse? They were not the same people who were brought out of Egypt and who saw all the miracles that God did in the wilderness!

You see, God's people were not brought out of Egypt on Monday night and into the Promised Land on Tuesday morning! Between verses 43 and 44, many things happened over a period of many years. And what happened was the difference between certain people living in the new land, the "lands of the heathen," and others dying in the wilderness. I don't know about you, but I don't want to die in the wilderness; I want to get to the land that God has for me!

So this first generation had the faith to get out of Egypt. They had the faith to be obedient when Moses said God had instructed them take their best, most expensive lamb and sacrifice it. They were to take the blood of the lamb and put it on the door and then eat the lamb from head to toe. It takes faith to eat every part of a lamb — eyeballs and everything! (*See* Exodus 12:1-20.)

This first generation also had the faith to go as slaves to the houses of their masters and demand that they give them gold, silver, and their best clothes for their exodus from Egypt (Exod. 12:36). Now in the natural, that makes no sense. If we look back just two hundred years ago to a time of slavery in America, we know that if some slaves went to their master's house and demanded his gold, silver, and clothes, they would end up severely punished.

But Israel heard from Moses that God said to do it, and they had enough faith to go ahead and actually do it. So these were people who knew how to walk and live by faith. When they came out of Egypt, they had the faith to walk through a sea. God rolled the water up on both sides and held it there like a wall of "JELL-O" while they walked through! I'm sure they were wondering, *When is this water going to fall?* Yet they had the faith to go through the Red Sea.

This was not a nation that knew nothing about faith or about following God. This was a nation of remarkable people. And yet, this nation didn't make it to the Promised Land. Why?

Let's read First Corinthians 10 to find out, because if we know where they went wrong, we won't make the same mistake.

1 CORINTHIANS 10:1
1 Moreover, brethren, I would not that ye should be ignorant, how that ALL our fathers were under the cloud, and ALL passed through the sea.

The word "all" includes everybody. Who's left after all? *No one!* So everybody came out of Egypt. Everybody experienced the miraculous deliverance. They were all under the cloud. They all went through the Red Sea. They all got into covenant with Moses and the Law. They all partook of the bread from Heaven. They all drank water from the rock. They all saw that God was great and that He would perform the miraculous to save them.

Let's read verse 5.

1 CORINTHIANS 10:5
5 But with MANY of them God was not well pleased: for they were overthrown in the wilderness.

These people who had enough faith to leave Egypt, enough faith to get riches, enough faith to receive healing, and enough faith to walk between two walls of water across the Red Sea were displeasing to God. That's kind of scary! Many of us are still working on our faith in the areas of finances or healing!

But these people had all of these blessings, yet God wasn't pleased with them. Why? Verse 5 says that they were overthrown in the wilderness. Satan took them out.

What Kept Israel Out of the Promised Land?

We can learn from Israel and not make the same mistakes that they made. Then we can enter our land — God's perfect will for our lives. You see, the Old Testament was written so that we can learn from it, so that we can learn from the mistakes people made as well as from the right things they did.

Let's continue reading in First Corinthians to find out how Satan took them out — what he did to overthrow God's people in the wilderness.

1 CORINTHIANS 10:6-12
6 Now these things were our examples, to the intent WE SHOULD NOT LUST AFTER EVIL THINGS, as they also lusted.
7 NEITHER BE YE IDOLATERS, as were some of them; as it is written, The people sat down to eat and drink, and rose up to play.
8 NEITHER LET US COMMIT FORNICATION, as some of them committed, and fell in one day three and twenty thousand.

**9 NEITHER LET US TEMPT CHRIST, as some of them also
tempted, and were destroyed of serpents.
10 NEITHER MURMUR YE, as some of them also murmured,
and were destroyed of the destroyer.
11 Now all these things happened unto them for ensamples:
and they are written for our admonition, upon whom the
ends of the world are come.
12 Wherefore let him that thinketh he standeth take heed
lest he fall.**

These are some of the things that the children of Israel did
that kept them out of the land. Let's look at each one of these in
more detail.

Number One: Lust

Lust stopped the children of Israel, and lust will stop you
from entering into your land and fulfilling God's perfect will for
your life. They lusted after things rather than searching after
God.

It's one thing to believe God for money, to believe that money
is coming. But it's another thing to go after money yourself. It's
one thing when money is chasing you down, but it's another thing
when you're chasing money down. That's why you don't play the
lottery. That's why you don't go to casinos. That's why you don't
get involved in get-rich-quick schemes.

It's one thing to be serving God, and God brings you that man
or woman of God to marry. Proverbs 18:22 says, "He that findeth
a wife, findeth a good thing." The word "findeth" implies that he
findeth her along the way. He is walking along the way fulfilling
God's will for his life, and, suddenly, there she is! That's the way
God intended it. He didn't intend for man to try to find his

woman, looking every which way he can and leaving God's will for his life in the process.

I'm talking about lusting after people and things. Israel lusted and it got them into trouble.

Number Two: Idolatry

The *second* thing they did was they got into idolatry. In other words, they made other things their god instead of God.

In another chapter, I talked about Joshua's faithfulness to follow Moses. You remember when Moses went up on the mountain to talk to God, Joshua was on mountainside waiting for him. Well, while Joshua was there, the nation of Israel took the silver and gold that God had given them and built calves. Then they worshiped the calves.

The nation of Israel had seen ten plagues come on Egypt. God had supernaturally brought them out with lots of money. They saw God part the Red Sea, and yet they decided not to worship Him, but to instead worship this metal image! We may think that is the dumbest thing in the world — that we would never do *that*!

Of course, what the nation of Israel did seems stupid and foolish to us today. But very often people today will worship the car God has given them. Or they'll worship the man or woman God has given them. They might worship their educational degrees or the achievements God has allowed them to accomplish whether they be in athletics, scholastics, or community honors. People worship all these things God has given them instead of worshipping God Himself, and they end up getting off-track.

That's what these people did, and God wasn't pleased with them.

What was the *third* thing that kept the children of Israel out of the Promised Land?

Number Three: Fornication

First Corinthians 10:8 says, *"Neither let us commit fornication, as some of them committed, and fell in one day three and twenty thousand."* I don't want to think about what would happen if God judged everybody on the planet who committed fornication today. There would be mass destruction! Well, this is what happened with them.

They committed fornication, and 23,000 of them dropped dead in one day. Sexual sin stopped them from reaching the Promised Land. Remember, this generation had the faith to get out of Egypt, to get riches, to walk through the Red Sea. Yet these faith champions didn't make it to God's perfect will for their lives. Almost none of them made it, and one of the reasons was fornication.

The Bible says, *"Flee fornication. Every sin that a man doeth is without the body; but he that committeth fornication sinneth against his own body"* (1 Cor. 6:18). When you commit fornication, you put your body at risk. You put your whole spiritual life at risk. You could actually die over this thing two ways, spiritually and physically.

You could lose it all over some "knucklehead" — someone who doesn't even love you and is not planning to be with you. You're just something they have for a little while. And you pass up God's plan — His promised land for you — for that. That's not smart. Those 23,000 people who died missed out on the Promised Land and all the blessings of God that went with it over trying to get immediate gratification for their flesh.

Number Four: Tempting the Lord

The *fourth* thing that can keep you from the will of God is tempting the Lord. First Corinthians 10:9 in *The Amplified Bible* says, "We should not tempt the Lord [try His patience, become a trial to Him, critically appraise Him, and exploit His goodness] as some of them did — and were killed by poisonous serpents."

Notice the phrase "exploit His goodness." Romans 2:4 says, "...*despisest thou the riches of his goodness and forbearance and longsuffering; not knowing that the goodness of God leadeth thee to repentance?*" Has God been good to you? Has God been patient with you? Has God been longsuffering with you, waiting for you to get it right? I know He has been that way with me. It is the goodness of God that leads us to repentance.

Now there are many believers who are misusing the grace of God and are using First John 1:9 as a credit card, in a sense. What I mean by that is, although they got saved, they are still living wrong. They're saved, filled with the Holy Ghost, and know the Word of God, but they have decided to live wrong. They have decided to do it for now. They say, "When I turn thirty-five or so, I'm going to get it right with God. But right now I'm going to have a little fun."

The Bible says that the goodness of God leads us to repent. People may have messed up over and over again, but God has given them the opportunity to get back on-track. But the day is coming when if they continue doing that, God will say, "My hands are off of them." And the enemy is going to come in and knock them out. The goodness of God leads us to repent, not to live any kind of lifestyle we want.

People say, "I've got my fire insurance. I'm not going to hell, so I'm all right." But if they live that way with that attitude long enough, they will find themselves going to hell. Those people are tempting Christ.

Although God had been good to the nation of Israel and had done many great things for them, every time He gave them a chance to get themselves right, they continued to do wrong. Eventually, they paid for their stubbornness; they never made it to the Promised Land, to God's perfect will.

Number Five: Murmuring and Complaining

First Corinthians 10:10 lists the *fifth* thing that Israel did that kept them out of the Promised Land: *"Neither murmur ye, as some of them also murmured, and were destroyed of the destroyer."*

Many people think that complaining is just a "little white sin." But, no! All sin is on the same level with God, because sin is *sin*! These people were constantly complaining because they didn't see the answer yet.

In Exodus chapters 15 and 16, we see that they walked out of Egypt, walked through the Red Sea, and started complaining about the fact that they couldn't find water. So God blessed them with water, and then they started complaining and talking bad about Moses because they couldn't find bread.

They started saying, "We should have stayed in Egypt." And they said these things over and over again. From the time they left Egypt on their way to the Promised Land, they complained and complained and complained. They kept saying, "This is not going to work out. This is stupid."

And I am sure that if you looked at some time in your life, even recently, you would find that you've opened your mouth and said some things like, "When is this going to work out, God? I did this, this, and this, and it still didn't happen. God, I was better off staying where I was." We have opened our mouths, and our words were against God.

In Malachi chapter 3, God told those in Israel that they had been tithing and giving offerings, all right, but that He had rejected them because they were complaining. They were saying, "I give to God, yet I don't get a return. I've been giving to God for six weeks, and I haven't gotten any return. He said that He would open the windows of Heaven, but He hasn't done it in my life. He hasn't done it yet, so I'm going to go back to what I was doing before." God reproved them and told them that their words were against Him. He said, "You need to start tithing again because complaining will always stop your blessing."

I know that in my life I've had many opportunities to complain. I have caught myself many times saying, "I don't know why You have me here, God. This is not working out. God, I did what You said to do. I don't know, I just give up." But, you see, this attitude is a trick of the devil to cause you to knock yourself out with your own words. That's what happened with Israel.

They always said to Moses, "Moses, you brought us out here to die in the wilderness!" And remember, you can have what you say (Mark 11:23). So they died in the wilderness! (*See* Numbers 14:27-35.) Was that God's plan? No, He had the Promised Land for them.

That thing right under your nose — your mouth — is either the most effective, productive thing or the most destructive thing in your life; it depends on how you use it. The murmuring of Israel kept them out of the Promised Land, even though it was God's perfect will for them to end up there.

These five things — *lust, idolatry, fornication, tempting Christ*, and *complaining* — are some of the sins that kept Israel out of the Promised Land. The enemy used these things to keep them out. And he will try to use these things to keep *you* from fulfilling God's will for your life.

There were two more things that kept the children of Israel from the Promised Land. And we find out what those were in the Book of Hebrews.

Number Six: Lack of Spiritual Growth and Progress

To get to your promised land, you have to go through the wilderness. In the Old Testament, the wilderness was a land of "just enough," where God's provision was always available, but it was just enough to sustain them until they reached the Promised Land, the land of "more than enough." When it comes to fulfilling God's will for your life, the wilderness is known as "preparation time." But it is not God's desire that the wilderness be a place to set up camp, so to speak. It's designed as a place to walk *through* on your way to your promised land.

The distance from Egypt to the Promised Land that God had given Israel was supposed to be an eleven-day trip. But Israel spent *forty years* there in the wilderness! Wow!

Let's look in-depth at this sixth reason why that generation of God's people never entered the Promised Land.

HEBREWS 3:7-10
7 Wherefore as the Holy Ghost saith, To day if ye will hear his voice,
8 Harden not your hearts, as in the provocation, in the day of temptation in the wilderness:
9 When your fathers tempted me, proved me, and saw my works forty years.
10 Wherefore I was grieved with that generation, and said, THEY DO ALWAY ERR IN THEIR HEART; AND THEY HAVE NOT KNOWN MY WAYS.

The Amplified Bible says, ". . . They always err and are led astray in their hearts, and they have not perceived or recognized My ways and become progressively better and more experimentally and intimately acquainted with them" (Heb. 3:10). What does that mean? They weren't growing in God. Very simply, if you aren't growing in God — if you're not moving forward — you are going backwards.

As Christians, we're in a war. We're not warring to win the victory that Jesus has already won. But we're warring to take what He did to a lost world. Well, in a war, you have to keep advancing against the enemy. You have to establish your dominance. Similarly, in a boxing match, if you're in the ring fighting against someone and you don't do what's necessary to move forward, your opponent is going to push you back.

You see, if you're not pressing into the things of God, the devil is pressing you back. There's no such thing as standing still. If you are not growing in God, you have backslidden.

Those Israelites who'd escaped from Egypt's bondage didn't do what was necessary to grow in God. Therefore, they had a problem. God said, *"So I sware in my wrath, They shall not enter into my rest"* (Heb. 3:11). Or we could say, "...They shall not enter into My Promised Land."

Then we as believers are admonished in the next verse to take heed: *"Take heed, brethren, lest there be in any of you an EVIL HEART OF UNBELIEF, in departing from the living God"* (Heb. 3:12). We can decide not to believe what God says, and if we do that, we are in sin. If you see that God has promised you certain things for your life if you obey Him, and you decide that you will not believe it, you are in sin.

Number Seven: Lack of Faith

Every step of the way into your promised land will be a step of faith. And in every situation, you have to make that step — and sometimes that leap — of faith or you're still in the wilderness. That's what happened with Israel. Their lack of faith kept them out of the Promised Land.

In Numbers chapter 13, we find that Israel finally got up close to the Promised Land. They sent twelve spies into the land. Ten of the twelve who came back said, "We can't take that land. There are giants there! Sure, the land is wonderful like God said, but we don't have enough people to take on those giants." So the whole nation began crying and bawling and squalling. They cried all night long. They cried because they didn't believe God could take out some giants for them when God had just taken out a nation for them!

God said, "That's evil. Where's your faith?" Jesus would often ask His disciples this same question. He would say, "Where is your faith? What's the matter with you?" Faith is a "substance" that God expects believers to walk in. He says that the just shall live by faith (Rom. 1:17) — not that the just should *consider* walking by faith. No, to walk by faith is a command.

A lack of faith is the biggest thing that kept Israel out of the Promised Land. They could not enter in because of unbelief. Hebrews 3:19 says, *"So we see that they could not enter in because of unbelief."*

God has promised you certain things. He told you that if you followed Him, He would bless you. If you follow Him, you will have "heaven on earth." If you do His work, there will be a reward. Right now it may seem as if you're suffering. You may not think you're having as much fun as somebody else. You may not be receiving all the money somebody else is getting or all the things the world has. But God said, "I told you that if you do things My way, you'll be blessed." Get in God's Word; get His Word in you so that you will be able to believe what He has said.

When God called me to RHEMA Bible Training Center, I had to believe that although I didn't want to go to Bible school, if I became willing and obedient to go anyway, God would bless me. I also knew that when certain obstacles came across my path, God expected me to have enough faith to get past them. So I used my faith and stood my ground. I didn't want to miss the promised reward!

There will always be "Red Seas" and "Jordan Rivers" in your way even as you're walking in faith and obedience. God expects you to have the faith and determination to go forward and get past them.

So we know that one reason the children of Israel didn't enter the Promised Land was a lack of faith. They considered the circumstances instead of considering the Word. And they died in the wilderness as a result, never having reached the Promised Land.

Did the Second Generation Make It to the Promised Land?

The first generation died out, not entering God's rest or God's Promised Land as He had said (Heb. 3:11). Let's look at the next generation.

JOSHUA 1:10-13
10 Then Joshua commanded the officers of the people, saying,
11 Pass through the host, and command the people, saying, Prepare you victuals; for within three days ye shall pass

over this Jordan, to go in to possess the land, which the Lord
your God giveth you to possess it.

12 And to the Reubenites, and to the Gadites, and to half the
tribe of Manasseh, spake Joshua, saying,

13 Remember the word which Moses the servant of the Lord
commanded you, saying, The Lord your God hath given you
rest, and hath given you this land.

In verses 11 through 13, Joshua is giving the people certain
commands. In effect, he said, "You're going to go over the Jordan
River." And if you continue reading, you will find out that they
did. They went through the Jordan River just as the first
generation went through the Red Sea.

This second generation was made up of the children of those
who went through the Red Sea. And God told this second
generation to take the land, as He had done with the first
generation before they repeatedly disobeyed and rebelled against
Him. Joshua reminded this younger generation of the word God
had given to Moses. And what was their response?

JOSHUA 1:16-18
16 And they answered Joshua, saying, ALL THAT THOU
COMMANDEST US WE WILL DO, and whithersoever thou
sendest us, we will go.

17 According as we hearkened unto Moses in all things, so
will we hearken unto thee: only the Lord thy God be with
thee, as he was with Moses.

18 WHOSOEVER HE BE THAT DOTH REBEL AGAINST THY
COMMANDMENT, and will not hearken unto thy words in
all that thou commandest him, HE SHALL BE PUT TO
DEATH: only be strong and of a good courage.

They said two things: First, they said they would do
everything they were told to do. (That was a change from their

parents' attitudes!) And, second, they said that anyone who rebelled would be killed. Now if this had been the case when their parents were alive, they would have ended up killing their own parents, because their parents rebelled against the word of the Lord. This generation decided they weren't going to make that same mistake.

Have you ever been on a sports team and heard the coach say, "Nobody is to be out after midnight"? If one person broke curfew and stayed out, the whole team had to pay the price the next day at practice, probably by running extra miles or by performing some other physically grueling task.

If that happened to your team, what would you be likely to do the next time you saw that one person who sneaked out past curfew? That person better hope the coach is nearby, because you'd probably want to hurt him!

Well, that's exactly what this second generation was saying in this passage of Scripture. They didn't want anyone keeping them from fulfilling God's will for their lives. They were not going to permit all of them to suffer for the disobedience of a few.

A Covenant of Their Own

After this generation passed through the Jordan River and was on their way to Jericho, the Lord said to Joshua, ". . . *Make thee sharp knives, and circumcise again the children of Israel the second time"* (Joshua 5:2).

Now all the people who had come out of Egypt were circumcised, but all the people who were born in the wilderness were not circumcised. They didn't have a covenant of their own yet. Their parents had a covenant because they had been circumcised, and we know that a covenant required their blood to be shed. And so, before God could do for this second generation what He wanted to, they had to have a covenant of their own.

This brings me to an interesting point. Just because your parents may have messed up — just because they may have stayed in the wilderness and didn't get to their promised land — is no excuse for you to just fold your hands and quit. You have no excuse for not following God. The covenant you have with God is not a covenant between your parents, you, and God. No, it's a covenant between you and God, period. And the covenant says that if *you* do what God says to do, He will bless *you*.

This scenario is often why preachers' kids are known as "hellions" — the worst group in the church. Some preachers' kids say, "My parents spent too much time in the ministry, and they didn't do enough for me, so I'm going to rebel against God." But *God* didn't shortchange them; their *parents* shortchanged them. Now the children are wanting to take it out on God. But, really, in so doing, these preachers' kids are only hurting themselves because they are falling short of God's perfect will and His best blessing for their lives.

Even if your parents didn't do the right thing — even if your parents put ministry before the family — that's no excuse for you not to follow God.

Did you ever notice that someone in the Bible had probably the worst father of all and yet chose not to follow his father's example? Jonathan's father was Saul. Saul was called of God, but an evil spirit drove him crazy. He went from being God's man to being a very terrible man who tried to kill David.

According to natural, fleshly thinking, Jonathan had every excuse in the world to be evil and conniving. Yet you'll find that he was one of the nicest, most loving, God-like people on the planet.

So it doesn't matter what your parents did. Everybody's parents miss it in some way or another. And if you don't have children yet, there will probably come a day when you will have children and make some mistakes of your own. You have to mature to the point of knowing that your parents did their best and that what happens in your life is not dependent upon what they did or didn't do, but upon what *you* do. Don't use your parents' failures as an excuse for not becoming successful in God.

This second generation of Israelites all had parents who had failed, yet they decided to take the good that their parents had done and incorporate that into their lives. And then they took the bad and made sure they didn't repeat it. As a result, they made it to the land God had for them.

What Did the Second Generation Do Right?

What was it that this second generation did that caused them to enter the Promised Land? The *first* thing they did was *to hate sin*. I didn't say they tiptoed up next to sin to see how close they could get to it without going all the way, so to speak. I said they *hated* sin! That means they stayed away from it!

There was a particular man in their camp by the name of Achan. Israel conquered Jericho, and God told them not to take as spoils certain things from Jericho. Well, Achan took what God said not to take; he disobeyed God. And they ended up losing their next battle because of his sin. When Israel found out what he had done, they stoned him to death. They weren't kidding when they said, "We'll kill whoever messes with our covenant!" (*see* Joshua 7).

The *second* thing they did was *to be obedient to the word of the Lord*. They were obedient to the man of God that God had placed in their lives — Joshua, the leader of the new generation.

The *third* thing they did was *to submit to Joshua's leadership.* Joshua 24:31 says, *"And Israel served the Lord all the days of Joshua, and all the days of the elders that overlived Joshua, and which had known all the works of the Lord, that he had done for Israel."* They served God and the nation all of Joshua's days.

The first generation didn't make it past a couple of days before they were serving golden calves instead of God. But this second generation served God all the days of Joshua's life. In everything they did, they operated in faith.

Let me give you just one example. In Joshua chapter 6, we find the story of how the walls of Jericho came down. Joshua, their man of God, said to walk around the city for seven days. He said that during the first six days, they were not to say a thing. But on the seventh day, they were to shout when he said, "Shout!"

So on the seventh day during the seventh time around the city, the walls were still standing as they marched. Those city walls were still wide enough for chariot races to be run on it, and, in the natural, shouting at the walls would only make them look stupid. But they had the faith to shout when the man of God said, "Shout!" They knew that he'd received that word from God. And they knew that if God said to shout and the walls would fall, they were going to shout and see those walls fall!

So they shouted, and when they did, the walls fell down. They ended up taking out seven nations that were as great as Jericho. They didn't do this with sword and spear or in their own strength or might. They did all this by faith.

Every step into your promised land will be a step of faith. Every step Israel took was a step of faith, and that's why they were successful. They believed the word of the Lord. Because they believed the word of the Lord, they saw miracles happen, and they entered into God's perfect will for their lives.

The Bible talks about how they were fighting a battle once, and they needed a little more daylight to win the battle. Joshua said, "Hey, God, stop the sun for a moment." And the sun actually stopped so they could continue to fight and win the battle! (*See* Joshua 10.) That's an absolute scientific fact. Israel had faith for miracles. They had faith for whatever it would take to get them into the land God had promised them.

The End Result of a New Generation's Faith

Let's read what the end result was for this second generation that followed God and did the things they were supposed to do.

> **JOSHUA 21:43-45**
> **43 AND THE LORD GAVE UNTO ISRAEL ALL THE LAND WHICH HE SWARE TO GIVE UNTO THEIR FATHERS; AND THEY POSSESSED IT, AND DWELT THEREIN.**
> **44 And the Lord gave them rest round about, according to all that he sware unto their fathers: and there stood not a man of all their enemies before them; the Lord delivered all their enemies into their hand.**
> **45 There failed not ought of any good thing which the Lord had spoken unto the house of Israel; all came to pass.**

God gave unto Israel — unto this second generation — all the land He had promised the first generation. They possessed it and dwelt therein. Remember, Psalm 105:43 says, *"And he brought forth his people with joy, and his chosen with gladness."* That's talking about that first generation of Israelites that God had led out of Israel. But the next verse, verse 44, is talking about their children some forty years later: *"And gave them the lands of the heathen: and they inherited the labour of the people."* The second generation inherited the fruit of what had been begun by the previous generation.

Every good thing God had promised His people when He delivered them out of Egypt was received by their children, the next generation. And the things that generation did to possess their Promised Land are the things we are to do today in order to possess our promised land.

Deuteronomy chapter 8 says that all their silver and gold was multiplied. Their flocks and their sheep were multiplied. Everything was multiplied! Deuteronomy chapter 28 says that they were blessed in the city, blessed in the field, blessed in the basket, blessed in the store, blessed going in, and blessed going out. They got into God's land — into His will for their life — and received all the blessings of God, not just a few of them.

That shows us that there are rewards for following God's plan. God has a plan for you. You will face challenges as you follow this plan. There will be steps of faith in this plan. There will be days when you will have the opportunity to be discouraged in this plan. But if you stick with it and stay with God, you will find that God has a greater reward for you than you ever thought possible.

Abraham started out as a normal guy with a wife who couldn't have a baby. He ended up as a very rich man with a son anointed by God. He became the father of many nations, and Jesus came from his seed. That was a spectacular reward that started with one step of obedience to leave his country and kinsmen to follow God.

Don't Be an 'In-and-Out' Christian — Be Faithful to God Each Step of the Way

You see, there's a journey from where you start to where you finish. In my own case, I started out as a high-school kid who was going to get a business degree, and I ended up as a minister and pastor in Smyrna, Georgia! I had to go through Bible school. I had to go through some training in Detroit. And I'm still following God's plan. But I'm already enjoying the benefits because I've been faithful to God. I'm not saying that I haven't missed it from time to time, but God is faithful, and as I dedicated myself each step of the way, He has always gotten me right back on-track.

When you're faithful to follow God's plan for your life, you'll find that there's a pot of gold at the end of the yellow brick road! In other words, at the end of the road called obedience is a place called prosperity. God has great plans for you. Right now, you're walking in part of His plan. And you may be facing certain challenges. But if you will just stay with God, you will receive His reward.

Proverbs 28:20 says, *"A faithful man shall abound with blessings: but he that maketh haste to be rich shall not be innocent."* The Kingdom of God isn't a get-rich-quick scheme. It's a lifestyle.

So who is a faithful man? He is a man who is reliable and steadfast — a man who won't be shaken when he comes up against adverse circumstances. He is a man who will stay with God's plan no matter what. He is a man who says, "I'm going to do what God says even if it kills me, although I know it won't!"

Proverbs 11:18 says, *"The wicked worketh a deceitful work: but to him that soweth righteousness shall be a sure reward."* God is not saying that you *might be* rewarded if you follow Him. He is not saying that if you follow Him, you *might be* blessed. God is saying that a day is going to come on this earth when you're going to say, "Look what the Lord has done!" But then God has something to say about another day when there will be a new heaven and a new earth. In other words, your blessings will ring out for eternity, in the world to come.

Fulfilling the plan and purpose of God for your life is the only race that I know of in which you run to get the prize from God at the finish line, but you are rewarded with prizes all along the way! You walk in God's blessings *while* you are fulfilling His plan for your life. And at the end, He says, "Well done, thou good and faithful servant. Enter into the joy of the Lord" (*see* Matthew 25:21).

When the world is pressuring you to do things its way, God says that there is a sure reward waiting for you if you will follow His plan. Others may say, "What you're doing is stupid. You should do it *this* way instead. It's more fun out in the world. There's no way you're going to make it doing things God's way all the time." But God has a plan for you. He wants you to have a heavenly life right now on earth, but you have to stay with Him to get there.

When you stay with God through the thick and the thin — when you walk through the valley of the shadow of death and you get to the other side of whatever you might be going through — you'll find that God has *too much* waiting for you! So stay with God and His plan. Believe what God says about you and what He says you're going to accomplish in Him. Hold fast in your heart to the blessing He says you'll walk in.

A Third Generation

We've already mentioned the first and second generations. But what about a third generation? I'm not talking about the physical descendants of those who entered the Promised Land. I'm talking about us, the Body of Christ. We are children of God and the Holy Ghost army of today! And this generation can be a third generation that obeys God and enters a land He has prepared for us.

Matthew 24:14 says, *"And this gospel of the kingdom shall be preached IN ALL THE WORLD for a witness UNTO ALL NATIONS; and then shall the end come."* Notice the words, "in all the world." We are called to reach the whole world! Our promised land is *the world* — world evangelism. And once we fulfill that, Jesus will come back and take us home.

I'm glad to be a part of this last day's army of God. We have more at our disposal than the Old Testament people of God had. We have God *in* us. We have the Word of God in our hands, and we can put it in our hearts. We can walk with God, talk with God, and live in His Presence.

Supply Your Part

Each one of us has a part to play in reaching the world with the Gospel of the Lord Jesus Christ. Let's read what the Apostle Paul said.

EPHESIANS 4:16
16 From whom the whole body fitly joined together and compacted by that which EVERY JOINT SUPPLIETH, according to the EFFECTUAL WORKING IN THE MEASURE OF EVERY PART, maketh increase of the body unto the edifying of itself in love.

Whether you're called to be a minister, a doctor, the owner of a music company, the President of the United States, or whatever it is, you are supplying your part when you fulfill that calling. You see, when you become what God has called you to be, you are placed in a position where you are doing your part in the Holy Ghost army. Your particular promised land means doing your part to win the lost in whatever vocation God has called you to.

Using a literal battle zone as an illustration, your part may be to be on the bridge shooting at the enemy. Your part may be to be on the frontlines running at the enemy. Your part may be to be someone in a tank running down the enemy. Whatever your part is, when you reach what God wants you to be, you can then start supplying. But you can't supply if you aren't where you're supposed to be, doing what you're supposed to be doing.

You see, "every joint supplying" as stated in Ephesians 4:16, works like the human body. It's hard to fight without a working arm, foot, or eye, for example. But when we each do our part, we function together as a whole, and we can effectively and efficiently avoid what Satan has for us and walk in what God has for us.

Don't be like the first generation that disobeyed God and rebelled against Him. Instead, do the things that the second generation did. They were a generation that walked with God and was obedient to Him. They stayed with God's plan. And, as a result, they entered their Promised Land. You, too, can enter your promised land and help take this planet for Jesus! Just take your place and start supplying!

As you serve God in your life — as you do what He has called you to do — you will be glorifying God individually. When the world looks at you, they will see the glory of God in your life. And as we do our part individually, we will be taking our places collectively as a generation taking the land and glorifying God.

Other Titles By Word of Faith Publishing

Bishop Keith A. Butler

A Seed Will Meet Any Need	BK003
Hell: You Don't Want To Go There	BK005
How To Be Blessed By God	BK013
Making Room for Yourself	BK007
Angels — God's Servants for You	BK010
The Last Week of Jesus	BK020
Success Strategies From Heaven	BK001 (Harrison House, Inc.)
What On Earth Are We Here For?	BK002 (Harrison House, Inc.)
Home Improvement (Bishop Keith A. Butler and Minister Deborah L. Butler)	BK029

Min. Deborah L. Butler

Establishing Godly Relationships Through Marriage and Family	BK012

Rev. Keith A. Butler II

God's Plan for the Single Saint	BK006

▶ The Internet. It has the potential to communicate information and connect people in powerful ways.

Now it is bringing together Kenneth Hagin, Kenneth Copeland, Keith Butler, Jesse Duplantis, Creflo Dollar, Jerry Savelle, Mac Hammond, and many more for something historic... something with exciting possibilities for you, your family, and the world.

THE TIME HAS COME

"Now you can join the online revolution, build your faith, protect your family and be a part of taking the Gospel to the world."

CFAITH.com
▶ YOUR INTERCONNECTED FAITH FAMILY

These well-respected ministries, along with many others, are uniting to connect the global faith family and reach out to others with the life-changing message of faith through the power of the Internet. They are coming together to launch **CFAITH.com**.